DOUBLE YOUR INCOME

STEPPING UP YOUR ACCOUNTING FIRM'S BOTTOM LINE

MARK LLOYDBOTTOM FCA

DOUBLE YOUR INCOME

Mark Lloydbottom, FCA

First Published 2016 by Marrho Limited © 2016

This book is published by Marrho Limited. No responsibility for loss occasioned to any person acting or refraining from action as a result of any material in this publication can be accepted by the author or publisher.

All rights reserved. No part of this publication, may be reproduced, stored in a retrieval system, or transmitted, in any form or by any means, electronic, mechanical, photocopy, recording or otherwise, without prior permission of the publisher.

ISBN: 978-1-908423-19-1

For further information visit www.marklloydbottom.com

Or to discuss how Mark can be of service please contact:

t:	+44 (0) 7767 872 278
e:	mark@marklloydbottom.com
w:	www.marklloydbottom.com
skype:	marklloydbottom

CONTENTS

Author ... 4

FOUNDATIONS
1. Introduction ... 6
2. Future accounting firm service model ... 10
3. Trends, benchmarks and insights ... 23
4. Snakes of complacency ... 36
5. Ladders of success ... 40
6. Strategic planning ... 48

DRIVING YOUR PROFITS UP
7. Firm and partner performance model ... 54
8. Your personal development and skill enhancement ... 67
9. The cost of poor service ... 70
10. Client meetings ... 74
11. Use an agenda ... 84
12. What do your accounts look like? ... 87
13. Raising the bar ... 96
14. Client care KPIs ... 104
15. Top line management ... 114
16. Agreeing prices with clients ... 117
17. The emerging role of the pricing director ... 126
18. Downsize your lock up ... 136
19. New billing and collecting horizons for today ... 140
20. Power up your gross margin ... 150
21. The cost of the ego trip ... 167
22. Core services ... 172
23. Specialist services ... 175
24. Profit enhancement strategies ... 180
25. Marketing ... 190
26. Final guidance and making it happen ... 206

Practice Management Academy -
Mark's Portfolio of Training Programs ... 216

AUTHOR

Mark Lloydbottom is acknowledged as a futurist who specialises in management planning and strategy for accounting firms. His programmes and consulting are based on over 30 years experience as a practitioner and consultant. He has worked with professional service firms in fifteen countries and has lectured throughout Europe, North America and Africa, standing on platforms with leading industry thinkers including David Maister and Paul Dunn.

Mark was a practitioner for 16 years having started his own practice in Bristol, UK in 1978. He is the founder of Practice Track and PracticeWEB and has also served on various committees with the Institute of Chartered Accountants, including the 2005 Working Party. Mark was a non-executive director of SWAT for ten years, serving as chairman for the last three.

He has worked closely with leading firms in the US including Practice Development Institute based in Chicago, BizActions in Maryland, AccountingWEB in the UK and USA and Faust Management Corporation in San Diego. He lectures throughout Europe, the United States and in South Africa for the Institute of Chartered Accountants of England and Wales, and the South African Institute of Chartered Accountants. Mark has lectured many times as a regular presenter for AccountingWEB at their annual management conferences both in the US and UK, and presented at the South African Accounting Academy at their inaugural Practice Management Conference. He also works with a number of the UK's leading firm associations, global accounting brands and accounting institutes.

He is devoted to researching and identifying strategies to enable accounting firms to build the top and bottom lines. He achieves this by delivering high-quality consulting, CD/DVD-based management training programmes and lecturing.

Mark is the co-author of Clients 4Life published by the Institute of Chartered Accountants of Scotland, South African Institute of Chartered Accountants and the Institute of Chartered Accountants of Australia and New Zealand. He is also the author of the CD/DVD/Manual Defining Edge, Deeper, Power UP Your Gross Margin, UPGRADE, Starting In Practice (SAICA), Double Your Income and firm-wide training programmes Delivering Outstanding Client Service and Better Billing, Better Collections. Lower Lock up. Guaranteed.

Apart from business interests, Mark enjoys cycling, is an active church member and founding trustee of Your Money Counts.

FOUNDATIONS

1 INTRODUCTION

The landscape for accounting firms changed significantly in the aftermath of the 2008 global financial crisis. Most have recovered and wonder perhaps what the next crisis might look like and when it will strike. Will the firm be robust enough to survive – and prosper? However, despite concerns over the past 25 years – whether as a result of competition, financial crises, recessions, changes in the demand for compliance services, Y2K or the technology empowerment of clients the fact is that most accounting firm owners have enjoyed good levels of increasing income.

If we add in concerns highlighted by the ICAEW's Tomorrow's Practice initiative which briefly came to the fore in 2015 and the general acceptance by practitioners that the landscape is changing then my views may be seen as having some conformity with those of others in the United Kingdom, Republic of Ireland, USA, South Africa (maybe to a lesser extent), Australia and New Zealand.

JOURNEY TO INCREASING PROFITABILITY

The promise on the cover of this book is that you can double your income – is this feasible? YES! It may take time but there is no doubt that you can join those who testify that they have doubled their income.

How?

Well, in simple terms there are only two ways to increase profitability – you either increase income – or reduce costs. Or both.

Increasing income – *"does that mean working harder?"* some ask. No, but working smarter, yes. It's about doing the right things as well as doing things right. It will almost certainly include charging more and stopping doing work for no reward. In Double Your Income we look at not just the possible strategies but also, perhaps more importantly, the possible strategic decisions to be considered in order to make that profit enhancement sustainable. The outcome depends on your determination to make that profit enhancement happen. Your results depend on many factors and we will look at some of those that will have the desired effect of enhancing profitability.

WHAT ARE THE KEY DRIVERS OF CHANGE IN THE PROFESSION?

To keep this straightforward, and avoid delving too deeply into the underlying drivers of change, some of these dynamics include:

New competitors

Recent years have seen new entrants into the accountancy marketplace.

The tax office: In Australia the tax authority works closely with technology companies enabling them to provide information direct so that certain tax filing requirements are automatically fed direct into the tax office and then transferred into pre populated forms.

In March 2015 the UK government announced to the amazement and perhaps the cynicism of the profession that the annual Tax Return was to be largely abolished while in December of that year a further announcement was made that digital tax accounts were to be launched for tax payers. By 2016 five million small businesses and ten million individuals will have access to their own digital tax account, and it is expected that by 2020 every individual and small business in the UK will have one.

The objectives? These must surely include advancing the payment of taxes.

The Big 4: Of the four largest brands three of them in the UK now provide online services to SME clients. Using technologies provided by companies such as Xero they provide an amazing array of real time services. KPMG in particular have invested heavily in their new SME small business accounting service offering; Deloitte work in the SME service sector with their service Propel by Deloitte.

Audit deregulation

Many countries have lifted audit thresholds. This has happened in Europe in particular as a consequence of European directives. A decade or more ago most companies in the UK required an audit. So, somewhere in the region of, maybe, 20,000 accounting firms were able to conduct an audit by virtue of their qualification and authorisation. In the UK the increase in the audit threshold has resulted in the population of audit firms reducing dramatically. Paradoxically, empirical evidence suggests that as audits have evaporated revenue from company clients has not diminished. But, audit revenue growth has all but ceased.

Tax deregulation

The UK differs from some countries in that small business owners owners whose gross business income is below the current VAT registration threshold are able to submit just totals of income and expenditure to the tax authorities – although they are still required to have accounts available. Tax returns can be completed and filed online and if that is not the case in your country – then be aware that online filing is probably top of someone's agenda be it government or the tax authorities. But taxation services remain the jewel in our crown and the accountant's office is where most people head when it comes to tax advice.

Financial statements preparation

This is undoubtedly a major source of revenue for accounting firms which has evolved slowly over the last five decades. Manual systems gave way to mechanisation followed by computerisation and then Cloud technology. We are not exactly the first industry to have our core service threatened by the advance of technology.

Clients do not usually have the time or inclination to attend to the finessing of their accounting records ensuring they are 'fit for purpose'. So, while Cloud technology appears in the 'threats' column it most definitely also appears in the one for 'opportunities' making it what I call a 'thropportunity' or an 'oppathreat.'

Technology, government and regulators

The reference above to Cloud technology naturally leads into the other external drivers of change and that is technology.

Since the 1980s when computerisation first enabled accountants to use technology in the office, information technology has evolved at an ever-increasing rate. Governments are capitalising on the online opportunities to enable computers to 'talk to one another' and exchange tax-driven information. The impact of technology coupled with deregulation means that the quantum of services emanating from compliance is in many countries withering on the vine. Where does it all end? In fact, while that is a question that accountants tell me they have asked it is in fact, I think, the wrong one. Why on earth wait until it is 'too late'? NOW, is the time to take action. In so doing, smart accountants will prosper and will be able to double their income.

Pricing

As we shall discuss the change to value pricing is already well under way. Most firms attest to the fact that the billable hour is all but dead. After all how many of your fee notes for the standard compliance service(s) change from year to year other than by the rate of inflation?

QUESTIONS TO ASK YOURSELF

1
What is the profit that you are aiming to add to your bottom line?

2
What has previously restricted your capacity for increasing profitability?

3
How open are you to focusing on consulting with your best client - your firm?

> **ASSESS** WHAT YOU NEED TO **ACHIEVE**.
> PLAN YOUR **STRATEGY** AND **IMPLEMENT**.
> **REVIEW** AND **ADAPT** WHEN NECESSARY.
>
> **MARK LLOYDBOTTOM**

2 FUTURE ACCOUNTING FIRM SERVICE MODEL

For the six decades I have been involved with the profession the first five can be characterised as being 'more of the same'.

The current decade is seeing more change than ever before – maybe more than in all those previous five decades combined. Clients are increasing able to use technology to deliver certain results, e.g. complete tax returns or prepare their own accounts. Government is increasingly requiring, or at least facilitating, online filing while the technology companies are busy delivering Cloud based applications to facilitate that objective. The accountant, in some scenarios is looking like the 'replaceable' middleman.

In some countries (e.g. UK and Australia) government is requiring less information. In the UK the government has announced that there will be less need for Tax Returns in the future while cash accounting enables most small businesses to deliver just the top line and bottom line results – not the full profit and loss account or balance sheet.

In some countries (e.g. South Africa and Ireland) more regulation has been introduced. But, the regulators infrastructure is considered inadequate at best while the regulation, of course, adds little or no value to clients.

THE [UK] HISTORY OF INSTITUTES REPORTING ON THE FIRM OF THE FUTURE

In 1997 the ICAEW and other Institutes published a 36-page consultation document report entitled, 'Added-Value Professionals'. This was followed up in January 2003 by a 32 page report entitled, 'The Profitable and Sustainable' Practice.

Both reports envisaged the oppathreat of technology and the Internet, the need to move on from being reliant on fees from compliance and to develop a range of other advisory/value-driven services.

HOW HAVE THESE REPORTS BEEN RECEIVED?

I think it is fair to say that the first report was better received in that it was the first one and comprised some challenging material for firms to digest. The second report reiterated much that was in the first.

HOW MANY FIRMS CHANGED AS A RESULT?

I do not know. But these reports probably accelerated the development process for some firms. Larger firms were probably already ahead on many aspects of the report recommendations. What I am certain of is that some firms failed to make changes. It wasn't that they did not try - it was more a case that there was no shortage of compliance work - clients were not queuing at the door for some of the new services that firms were seeking to sell clients.

LESSONS LEARNT

I think the major lesson that has relevance today is that firms succeed when they:

- Bring in a specialist who is dedicated to a particular service, or
- Develop a range of advisory services that can be seen as small step services on from the compliance relationship, that

    Meet a current need, and

    Deliver a ROI – not just alluding to one

Sometimes when I am lecturing about developing new services accountants tell me that they, *"do this work but don't charge for it."* So how to address that issue?

A STRAIGHTFORWARD APPROACH

Decide what your main 5-10 extension (a range of small step services that are natural follow ones from compliance) services are. Make sure you have the systems (letters, spread sheets etc.) so you can deliver these cost effectively. Create your marketing material (brochure cards/newsletters and so on). Make sure these services feature on your website and promotional material in your reception. Determine the price starting point – yes the dreaded - prices from...

Make sure you develop a plan to promote these to your top 20 clients and introduce them at the outset to:

- Your advocates (banks, solicitors, clients who are happy to refer you and so on)
- All your new clients

Finally make sure your staff know about your [extended] services and look for opportunities to refer leads to you. Some of these services should also be ones that your staff can get involved with – in identifying which services clients need and maybe also in the delivery of these services.

FUTURE ACCOUNTING FIRM SERVICE MODEL

			DRIVERS	RISK	REWARD
AUDIT	ACCOUNTS	TAXATION	Price Timeliness Best results	Insured Loss of client	Recurring fees Compliance advocacy
ONE SMALL STEP					
WEAKNESSES/ SYSTEMS	WHAT DOES IT MEAN? NEXT YEAR?	ASSURANCE OF TAX MINIMISATION			
STEPPING UP			Value/R.O.I End results	Loss of client	Relationship impacting present and future Higher value – higher price
[NEW] ASSURANCE SERVICES	UPDATING FINANCIAL REPORTING	TAX PLANNING			
TOP FLOOR			Relationship Confidence F.D. expertise	Loss of trust/ confidence/belief	A journey of risk and reward – challenge – personal growth Satisfaction in job well done
Key strategic partner. Coach. Business solution provider on-demand. A face-to-face relationship focused on the present and future.					

COMPLIANCE

ADVISORY

PERPETUAL

FUTURE ACCOUNTING FIRM SERVICE MODEL

As a consequence of working on the various ICAEW Future of the Accounting Firm Committees – there have been three and I have been involved with them all – I have come to certain conclusions…

We can employ hindsight to look back at the prevailing marketplace following the publication of these reports. The first two were timely but perhaps, in certain regards, were ahead of their time for the intended audience. The reality is that while there were fewer audits following the introduction of an audit threshold in 1999 at a level of £350,000 there was little evident diminution in the flow of on-going compliance work and new clients abounded.

LEVERAGE HAS REDUCED

However, from 1997 (the date of the publication of the first report) there has been a noticeable reduction in firm leverage (the number of professional staff employed per firm owner). In 1997 this was around 12-15 per partner – occasionally more and sometimes less. However by 2016 this reduced to between 8-11 – again, sometimes more and sometimes less. And during this period firm owners report that they have rarely been busier which is interesting because this is not necessarily evidenced by the trend in chargeable hours, which for many firm owners has charted a somewhat southerly course.

So, there was no shortage of firm owner work but maybe that is not the full reason why accountants struggle with doing non-compliance work. Some of the other factors include:

1 Risk

I am not looking here at the risk that can be insured against through professional indemnity policies. I am referring to the risk that if the accountant does not perform well in this area then the client may go elsewhere for their compliance work.

By definition most, if not all, non-compliance services revolve around peering into the future. What tax planning should be actioned? What course should be charted for the business? What is the value of the business? Any service that takes a look into the future must, by definition involve making assumptions – the state of the market, future tax changes and so on. Making assumptions and advising in these areas involves risk and accountants tend to be risk-averse.

2 Policies, systems and procedures

Firms have systems, policies and procedures to enable them to deliver compliance work. However, non-compliance work (or extension services as I often call them) often involves starting from square 1 with very few templates and a likely high involvement of partner and perhaps manager time. So, the average cost in terms of hours tends to be higher for firm owners who are accustomed to valuing their time and advice at premium rates for compliance services.

3 Selling

Not most accountants' favourite word. A compliance service, if performed to the client's satisfaction does not need to be sold over and over again. Sell once; delivery over [many] years is the panacea for accountants. Not so with extension services as they often need to be sold on each occasion.

4 Value

While many insist they deliver value the reality is that compliance services solve a problem in enabling clients to meet their filing and tax assessment requirements. Along this journey there is the opportunity to impress clients with tax planning advice or business advisory skills.

The ultimate evidence as to whether a client is happy with any non compliance services is not the payment of the account but the client returning for more of your other services!

5 Lack of expertise

Do you have the expertise coupled with the confidence to deliver services beyond compliance? Some firms have succeeded by recognizing their limitations and have not felt the necessity to commit to extending the firm's core skills platform. I have one client in the south east of England who, when he saw the opportunity to advise on estate planning and estate taxes committed five days to attending courses and over 100 hours studying. This was then followed up by advising some smaller clients before turning his attention to the firm's larger clients. The results? In year 1 he devoted over 150 hours to advising clients and year 2 - 225 hours – all at premium rates.

6 Unwillingness to invest in bought in expertise

In the 1970s the managing partner of Solomon Hare (a Bristol, UK firm with about 200 partners and staff at the time) invested in two specialists – on day 1 there was no book of business for their service skills and so the salary costs were absorbed while partners recommended their new specialists and they, in turn, started networking around the city boundaries – and beyond. The results? The firm grew exponentially partly as a consequence of the higher expertise and the firm's higher profile.

7 Water down the path of a mountain always follows the path of least resistance

Life tends to be lived according to the highest level of priorities and for many this remains the compliance work. Not surprising given that filing deadlines and penalties lie around every corner – and so many clients do not deliver the required records in time for this work to be completed.

Like water down the mountain – the path of least resistance is the compliance work, of which, hitherto there has been an abundance. Why do one off work with all the attendant risks and responsibilities when you can process compliance work through the office?

8 Lack of service profitability

Curiously, some accountants have told me that because of the high level of senior time required to deliver such services the profitability of this work is an issue. To which my response is that it might be the case that more confidence in the pricing of such work and better systems and processes might reduce the time to deliver. So invest in doing all you can to ensure that you have systems policies and templates in place. You also need to move on from fear – fear of losing the client because you have quoted a higher fee than you think the client will accept. Be confident in your own ability and your value. Can you frame a proposition to the client that enables them to understand that in investing in your fee they will make a greater gain than the cost?

Incidentally, whenever introducing a client to any service beyond compliance it is essential to be able to present the value proposition to the client. Why should they pay you unless they fully understand what the gain is to them?

YOUR GOODWILL BANK BALANCE

Michael Gerber in his excellent book The E Myth introduces the concept of emotional capital. What is emotional capital? I like the way that Clate Mask and Scott Martineau describe this in Conquer the Chaos, *"Emotional capital is the currency you use to wake up every day and fight the battle. It's the passion, enthusiasm and positive outlook that propel you through your day, keeping you driven to achieve your goals."* If you don't make deposits to your emotional capital account, the next thing you know, you're living in chaos — the ambition and drive you had to have a successful business is wearing thin, and your business is running you! ...

This led me to consider how this might apply to the accountant–client relationship. You have served the client for years and during that time you have built trust and credibility with the client. There is a bond of trust as a result of your excellent service and great advice. You have built a bond that is often referred to as goodwill so think of this as your goodwill capital balance or goodwill 'bank' balance. The first time you make a mistake, unless it is very serious, the client does not immediately rush off to another accountant, but there may well be a debit to your goodwill bank account with that client. But the account is not overdrawn so the client forgives and continues to engage you as the accountant.

So, looking back at those services, what do your clients need – which may differ from what you wish or are able to offer.

Will this improve your profitability?

Yes. Not only will you earn higher fees from clients you will be developing a service that combines compliance with advice that impacts clients today and tomorrow. Higher visibility. Higher level of service. Higher value. For you – higher level of job satisfaction. Higher level of personal challenge. Higher likelihood of client referrals and higher fees, of course.

BUT WHAT ABOUT CLIENTS?

The above provides a long list of reasons why accountants have not succeeded – you may recognise some of them, perhaps not all.

When the first Added Value report was published there were a number of companies that endeavoured to sell added value services to accountants such as Boot Camp (a service portfolio developed by Rick Payne and Paul Dunn), Profit Plus – a profit improvement service developed by Practice Track in conjunction with Reeves and Neylan. These turnkey solution services were then followed by two UK organisations – Added Value Network, developed by Steve Pipe and 2020 developed by Gordon Gilchrist, Ian Fletcher and Chris Frederiksen.

As I was involved with the development of Profit Plus for Practice Track I think I learnt along with the firms who subscribed to the system that there are not necessarily a long line of clients lining up for any additional service you plan to sell them.

The key is to use the power of agenda (this will be discussed in a later chapter) and your diagnostic questions that seek to explore what problems and issues the client has and then seek to address those. That is a much lower hurdle for a client to overcome than if you seek to sell them your latest packaged service.

WHAT IS THE FEE POTENTIAL?

We need to start by looking at what you have billed clients for this type of work in the last 12 months. The proposition that you

What additional services have you 'sold' in the last 12 months?

Client	Fees in last year	Compliance fees	Services bought	Services introduced/sold

Let's start with some diagnostics to establish the current situation:

Client

Enter up the name of client.

Fees in last year

The total of this column will be equal to your total firm revenues for the last year.

Compliance fees

For each client enter the fees charged that relate to compliance. If any invoice refers to any service that you regard as non-compliance you must still analyse it as compliance as so far as the client is concerned they will have regarded this as your routine compliance work. Further, so you have not felt able to separate out the fee separately you may have decided that you did not wish to draw attention to this extra cost. Okay, I understand that for tax purposes you may have decided to roll this into one fee, but nevertheless the analysis should remain as compliance.

Services bought

If, as a result of the client's circumstances your client has 'bought' services from you then these fees should go into this column. For example, the client may have been charged for a tax investigation or they have bought or sold a business. Their situation has resulted in then asking for your help as the accountant.

Services introduced/sold

Now, why the terminology? Not all accountants like to think of themselves as salespeople. The excuse that *"I am a professional not a salesperson"* might even be heard on occasions. But as professionals it is important to introduce clients to our various solutions targeting our introductions to services that meet the expressed or perceived needs of the client. It is of paramount importance that we do not underserve clients or allow clients to go to another service provider because they did not know of the range of services you could provide.

> **Key point:** Our role as accountants is to be solution providers.

So, what is the value of this column? The likelihood is that this is a column that is massively under populated. What are the services that you offer that can help solve client problems? How do you price? What systems, processes and templates do you need to create to enable you to seamlessly deliver value and profit?

YOUR SERVICE OFFERING – WHERE TO START?

Please refer to the Service Extension table in the last chapter of this book-Marketing (page 191).

This requires you to follow three steps:

1   Identify your top 20 clients

You will have your own criteria for making this selection. It could be by size of fee; turnover; quantum of balance sheet assets; clients that may be in your specialist sector or even the ones who recommend your services.

2   Decide on your five extension services

There is no magic bullet embedded in the number five, but I find that it is a small number to relate to and, surprisingly for some, this in itself requires a measure of stretch to identify five services that can be offered beyond compliance.

One test to apply is to add in a qualifier that you should only include services that have been delivered during the preceding year unless you are confident that there is a demand and you can deliver.

One key is to endeavour to include services that are appropriate for 80 per cent of your client portfolio.

Agree these among the owner group – dependent on the expertise among the owners this list may differ from one partner to another. However, this also identifies areas where one owner could introduce another.

You should be clear on what problems these services promise to solve. Do you have a range of fees in mind for each service? Do you need to create engagement letters, pro formas, templates for reports and so on?

3   Service grid diagnostics

With the table complete you now need to move on to identify which services have already been delivered. Enter a symbol such as a tick. You should also consider whether a specific service needs to be repeated or updated. Those services that are not applicable for a particular client you will enter a symbol such as a cross. Then for those clients where you have already introduced the service enter a symbol such as an i.

When this diagnostic exercise is complete you may have as many as 60 to 80 per cent of the 100 cells empty. This is your starting point for extending your service to existing clients.

HOW TO INTERPRET THE FUTURE FIRM SERVICE MODEL

So, with the introduction complete let us look in more depth at the Future Accounting Firm Service Model.

How to succeed and how to evolve?

It might seem obvious but the good news is that you should allow your service proposition to develop from your core trilogy of compliance services. Here you have a captive audience just like the dentist who is entitled to see the patient in the surgery every three or six months.

However, one practitioner I met at a seminar looked at the list of core services in chapter 22 and made the comment, *"We deliver all of these services, but the problem is we don't charge for any of them!"*

I thought, *"Why? Why would you not recognise your value."* Sadly he spoke to me in a resigned manner with seemingly little intention to change. Maybe registering as a charity? Ouch.

COMPLIANCE

So, the first lesson is to ring fence the service component of our three services and not use these as a platform to launch into displaying all our higher level expertise when in compliance mode. That is what I refer to as the peacock syndrome. It is the desire to impress clients that results in the provision of gratuitous advice.

The compliance service should comprise:

The delivery of the service, and a one small step service:

1. The audit – systems advice
2. Accounts – the accounts and what do they mean and what to do next
3. Taxation – restrict your input here to the basics of business tax. Taxation is the jewel in the accountant's crown and should not be given away or under valued.

ADVISORY MEETING

The key in the compliance meeting is to engage with clients to identify where the issues are and how you can be of service. Clients come to your office to address the matters appertaining to the compliance work. When this is finished they leave your office and probably immediately check their mail and incoming calls – the meeting with you is already receding into the background. So, use any time you have to find out the areas of pain and then set up a separate meeting. The advantage of this approach:

- The client will be able to do any research and provide any information you may require
- The client may need to bring along a spouse or work colleague
- The client is likely to take your advice more seriously in that is not just added into the compliance meeting
- You can undertake the research necessary for the meeting, and importantly
- You can agree a fee with the client for this additional service.

STEPPING UP

Audit

I was involved Robert K Elliott (at the time the second most influential partner in KPMG, USA) who was the Chair of the AICPA Future of Assurance Services Committee. In 1996 this Committee was responsible for recommending the introduction of two new services: 1) Elder Care and 2) Webtrust. Heard of them? Probably not. And if you have what revenues do these services generate?

The point is that I don't believe that SMPs are likely to be able to generate any additional fees from audit work other than that which is mandated by law or regulation. You will have your own view on the potential of future audit revenues.

Accounts

Can you offer clients a service that moves closer to real time accounting services?

> Flash reports
>
> Management accounts – monthly or quarterly
>
> Where clients have Cloud based accounting – can you help them interpret information and provide reports?

Taxation

The reason for restricting advice on taxation in compliance services is to avoid donating your high quality advice to clients. Advice on capital tax planning, estate planning, VAT...

PERPETUAL SERVICE

I know a number of accountants who offer their clients an on-going advice service. This normally involves meeting with clients 4-6 times a year – sometimes more. These accountants tell me they have a close relationship with these clients providing something akin to a FD type service. These accountants have developed management expertise in addition to their compliance expertise. They have a deep understanding of business issues and can bring insight into the client's business making decisions. But let me stress they all acknowledge they don't have all the answers – far from it. What they have is an ability to challenge the client's mindset, suggest options, where necessary recommend other solution providers. They also act as accountability partners – they encourage clients to stretch. They stand on the sidelines cheering and congratulating success and empathising when failure comes along.

I know one partner who has more than one hundred such relationships – why not you as well?

DRIVERS, RISK AND REWARD

The final component of the future accounting firm service model. The model is largely self explanatory and emphasises that compliance work increasingly requires work to be completed on a timely basis while advisory work requires the client to be able to touch and feel the return on their investment in your charges plus their time and effort.

The risk beyond compliance is that an unhappy client may well not return for their compliance work but as you move toward the perpetual FD role there is much greater reward in terms of client satisfaction – provided you maintain the trust and the confidence of the client.

QUESTIONS TO ASK YOURSELF

1
What is your view of the future of your revenues
from compliance services?

2
Can you identify clients who may well be interested
in buying your advisory services?

3
Can you identify three or more clients with whom you
could advance the proposition of a more structured relationship
that goes way out beyond compliance services?

4
£££ action – What can you do differently and what impact
will that have on your profitability?

> THE **THREE** INGREDIENTS FOR A **REMARKABLE** ACCOUNTING **FIRM**.
> "**LOOK** GREAT. **SOUND** GREAT. **BE** GREAT."
>
> MICHAEL CARTER, PRACTICE PARADOX, AUSTRALIAN MARKETING FIRM

3 TRENDS, BENCHMARKS AND **INSIGHTS**

LET'S LOOK AT [SOME] TRENDS IN THE PROFESSION

The basis for this material are surveys published in the USA by Mike and Kelly Platt of Inside Public Accounting. These surveys are based on responses from more than 500 firms of all sizes. For the purposes of providing information that will be of value I have included benchmarks that I consider apply to firms with revenues of between £1 and £15 million.

But before we progress, a reminder that this is one business (aka as a profession) where there are very few standards in performance.

All references are made on the basis that the survey results are always presented and interpreted on an 'apples for apples basis' – so the impact of mergers does not distort the results.

1 Organic revenue growth

What firms are achieving? On average firms currently grow thereabouts to 5 per cent above the rate of inflation with very few firms achieving somewhere in the 30% region while about 15% of firms turned in negative performance.

Trends? Growth rates have marginally increased over the past few years.

Key questions:
1. What have you achieved in the last five years – net of inflation?
2. What could you realistically stretch to achieve in the next 12 months?
3. What does this look like? What has to be done to achieve that growth rate?

2 Revenue per chargeable hour

What is your revenue per chargeable hour?

Revenue per charge hour formula:

<u>Net fees</u>
Charge hours

An increasing number of firms now earn fees from services that are not necessarily measured by the chargeable hour. These include services such as wealth management fees, M&A success fees and computer sales with these accounting for maybe as much as 10% of fee income.

Key revenue per chargeable hours questions:

1. What have you achieved in the last five years?
2. What could you realistically achieve?
3. How often will you monitor this performance?
4. What services do you or are you able to develop that are not based on the chargeable hour?

3 Revenue per employee

Of all the metrics that can be tracked, this is one that I think is of particular importance. Some metrics can, at best, be ambiguous, and at worst downright misleading. For example, revenue per partner – how are non-equity partners accounted for? Revenue per professional can also be defined differently by different firms. Are para-professionals included? Partners?

A good approach, applied consistently looks at the number of full time employees (FTE) on the basis of defining FTEs as including fee earning staff including partners, paraprofessionals and part-time staff (calculated based on the proportion of their time compared to a full week).

The revenue per employee will typically depend on your countries economy and firm salaries. Some of the primary factors affecting this metric include:

- Reduced fees due to client pressure for lower fees
- Partners' willingness to demand what is perceived by the firm as a fair and economic fee
- Market place competiveness, for example in the area of proposals
- Staffing for growth

4 The shrinking profit margin

Remember the days of one third, one third, one third? That is one third of revenue was accounted for by salary, one third overhead and one third was profit. For most firms those margins are now consigned to history.

- What is your margin?
- What are you doing to increase it?

This is referred to again in 7 below.

5 HR costs as a percentage of the top line

Staff costs have increased including the cost of salary, benefits, training (time and money), maternity and paternity leave, holidays and 'bank' holidays.

Firms in some countries report that staff performance is the biggest issue they face.

Worryingly, many firms are now reporting staff costs approaching and sometimes breaching the 50% of revenue barrier. Include a market-based salary for partners and how does your cost of salaries compare with gross revenues? What did this look like five years ago? Importantly, what can you do to improve profitability and reduce the cost of salaries?

What are your HR costs? The percentage of HR to gross fees must be monitored and any upward trend reversed. It is highly unlikely your firm's profits will increase unless this happens.

6 IT cost as a percentage of the top line

This has increased dramatically with technology companies typically charging for software on a per seat cost. Hardware and software require constant updates along with that the cost of training and developing competencies.

7 Fee resistance

Clients are more fee resistant than ever before.

So what are your current fee trends? What is your margin? All the benchmarking reports I have seen include graphs with margin showing a downward trend. These trends still show the most profitable firms generating a profit margin of 33% but firms in the lower range are reporting an average margin in the 25% region.

Key questions:

1. What has been your profit margin over the last 5 years?
2. What does your strategic plan envisage?
3. What does the new norm for your profit margin look like?

8 Net income per equity partner

When the global financial crisis struck in 2008 it did not take too long for firms to start saying goodbye to staff that were considered surplus to requirements. This exiting of resources also extended to partners with some who were close to retirement taking the decision, maybe with more than a little help, to vacate their desks while others were simply shown the door. The consequences? In many cases net income per equity partner increased.

How has this happened while clients have remained price conscious? How has this happened when many firms report struggling to find the right talent? There is, of course, more than one reason and reasons will vary from one firm to another. Factors include:

- Gaining more clients than have been lost
- Merging and gaining the advantages of lower overhead per unit of revenue
- Developing niche and non traditional services

What should net income per partner look like? I have seen this vary from as little as £7,000 for a [full time, 3000+ hours p.a. sole practitioner] to £500,000 average for a 10 partner firm.

What is your country's average pay? Multiply this by 5.5 as your first benchmark comparison with your own performance. Certainly your profits should exceed that.

9 Time on

When I first became involved in consulting time on (chargeable hours) for partners looked like 1200 hours in the USA and about the same in the UK.

Drift. How times have changed.

Today in some countries time on has drifted south to less than 900 while in the UK partners average thereabouts to 850.

I sometimes tell the story of one client firm whose managing partner (900+ chargeable) instructed me to consult with the firm. One of my briefs was to coach a partner whose performance had reduced to 450 charge hours a year. During my coaching time I managed to help him nudge his hours moving in the right direction, albeit only by a small increment. After consulting for three years we agreed the firm had made significant advances and they were now on the right path. Some three years on I met up with the managing partner and during the course of our conversation I mentioned that I was telling this one story about his partner who only accounted for 450 client hours. He smiled and said, *"Yes, I know, but let me ask you to guess how many hours he is doing now."* My guess was wrong – time on is now down to 350.

10 Non equity partners (aka salaried partners)

The traditional model of automatically making an upcoming manager is, I think, long since dead in the water. For firm profitability to be sustainable there is going to have to be a further shift which most likely will look like one equity partner to one non equity partner.

Where are we at now? I do not have the answer to that for the UK but in the USA 66% of reporting firms have non-equity partners. Typically non eqs. do not have the same capital requirement or the same levels of risk. However their time on and contribution is within reach of the equity partners. Their net income is maybe half that of the equity partners – maybe even less.

11 Where do new partners come from?

Typically 60% are promoted from the firm's talent pool and 40% are lateral hires from another firm.

12 Partner reviews

Typically only 50% of firms have a partner review process. So, you have reviews for all staff but when someone reaches the Holy Grail the review process defaults to partner meetings and maybe MP coaching?

13 What is the average age of the partner group?

Accountancy Institutes in the USA, UK and South Africa all report and have concerns that so far as those in practice is concerned this is an ageing profession. Your next partner decision – will this reduce your firm's average partner age?

14 What are the primary service sectors?

After auditing, accounting and tax services firms derive income from a range of other services. The following represent service specialisations that account for the 20% of firm revenue derived from non-compliance work.

Business valuations	0.5 - 1.6%
Business advisory services	1.6 - 5%
Computer consulting	0.6 - 4%
Fee based financial services	0.5 - 3.4%
Commission based financial services	0.1 - 3%
Health care	0.1 - 2.5%
Litigation support	0.3 - 2.2%
M&A	0.1 - 0.8%
Employee benefit admin	0.1 - 1%
HR consulting	0.1 - 0.5%
Other	2.5 - 11.8%

15 Lock up

Debtor average days	55
WIP average days	25
Total lock up	80 days

16 Percentage of billing rates compared to equity partners

Equity partners	100%
Salaried partners	95%
Profession staff with 9+ years of experience	70%
Professional staff with 6-8 years of experience	55%
Professional staff with 3-5 years experience	45%
Professional staff with 0-2 years experience	35%
Para professionals	30%

This benchmarking might help you review your staff charge rates.

17 Utilisation

Auditing and accounting	1300 - 1500
Taxation	1300 - 1400
Firmwide	66 - 72%

18 Staff hours

Professional staff hours	1900 - 2100
Professional staff hours billable	68 - 88%
Average charge hours – non-professional staff	200

19 Charge hours per professional staff

0-2 years experience	1350 - 1500
3-5 years experience	1500 - 1700
6-8 years experience	1400 - 1500
9+ years of experience	1200 - 1500
Paraprofessionals	1200 - 1400
Other staff	900 - 1400

20 Equity partners

Equity partner charge hours	900 - 1200
Equity partner total hours	2200 - 2400
Percentage total firm charge hours	7 - 27%

21 Non equity partners

Non equity partner hours	900 - 1400
Non equity total hours	2000 - 2200

22 Leverage

That is the number of staff a firm owner is managing, including themselves.

Normally in the range of 8 to 12 largely dependent on the extent to which the firm has audits.

23 What factors are taken into account when splitting the profit pie?

Charge hours delivered compared to budget	80%
Excess billable hours	70%
Goals and objectives met	75%
Management duties	90%
Marketing initiatives	50%
Originating new business	90%
Realisation rate	88%
Soft skills	50%
Teamwork	65%
Technical skills	65%
Training / mentoring staff	50%

24 What approach do you take in determining partner profit sharing?

Open system	70%
Closed system	30%
Formula system	50%
Partner group decision	10%
Profit sharing committee	15%
MP decides	12%
Other / combination of all	14%

25 Partner retirement

Do you have a plan for partner retirement?	65%
Is the plan fully funded?	10%
Is the plan partially funded?	68%

26 Average partner age   52

27 Do you have a mandatory retirement age?

Yes	64%
No	36%

28 If you have one – what is it?

Over 65	25%
65	70%
Under 65	5%

29 How many firms have terminated a partner?   34%

30 New partners

Lateral hires	55%
Non-equity partners admitted	45%

31 Capital required

Average capital required	£100,000

32 Average length of time to partnership

Less than 8 years	12%
8-10 years	20%
10-12 years	21%
12-15 years	32%
More than 15 years	15%

33 Requirements for admitting new partners

Yes	80%
No	20%

34 Requirements for admitting non-equity partners
Yes	68%
No	32%

35 Formal training program for current partners
Yes	88%
No	12%

36 Written partner performance reviews
Yes	96%
No	4%

37 Do you have a partner code of conduct?
Yes	84%
No	16%

38 Do you have a signed partner agreement?
Yes	100%

39 Do you use upward evaluations?
Yes	80%
No	20%

40 Do you use 360% degree reviews?
Yes	76%
No	24%

41 Does the firm have a firmwide strategic plan?
Yes	96%
No	4%

42 Does the firm have a departmental strategic plan?
Yes	68%
No	32%

43 Does the firm have a disaster recovery plan?

Yes	88%
No	12%

44 Does the firm have a marketing plan?

Yes	88%
No	12%

45 Does the firm have a succession plan?

Yes	72%
No	28%

46 Is there a written firm vision?

Yes	96%
No	4%

47 Are there written formal client acceptance guidelines?

Yes	96%
No	4%

48 Are there written core values?

Yes	96%
No	4%

49 Revenue per square foot   £280-£500

50 Costs as a percentage of firm revenues

Personnel	40-50%
Marketing	2%
Technology	3.5%
Recruitment	0.5%
Training/CPD costs	1%

51 Firm capital: How has this changed in the past 12 months?

Increased	20%
Remained the same	76%
Decreased	4%

52 Professional staff by years of experience

Equity partners	10%
Non-equity partners	5%
9+	16%
6-8	14%
3-5	17%
0-2	21%

53 Staff ratios

Professionals per admin staff	5
Professionals per equity partner	10

54 Turnover

What is staff turnover?	14%
Voluntary	77%
Involuntary	23%

55 Staff training

Do you have a formal mentoring programme?

Yes	88%
No	12%

56 Do you have a formal training programme?

Yes	100%

57 Do you have a business development director?

Yes	40%

58 Do you have an IT director?

Yes	80%

59 Do you have an HR director?

Yes	80%

60 Do you have a marketing director?

Yes	80%

61 What benefits do firms offer?

Pension plan contribution

Adoption benefits

Maternity leave

Paternity leave

Computer purchase programme

Domestic partner benefits

Health care

Life assurance

Flexitime

Gym membership

62 What do successful firms invest [aka budget] in marketing?

There is a range of essential ingredients and finance is only one of them. Here again there are no evident standards.

Marketing is about investing in the future of the business, creating a flow of new business that will, hopefully enable the business to grow.

I have one client with gross fees in the region of £600,000. For three years they hired a business development director at a cost of £60,000.

I also know some firms who have no marketing budget.

In the 30 or more years I have been involved in the profession I have followed the line that 'typically consultants to the profession recommend a marketing spend in the region of 3% of gross fees.' The Big 4 are believed to spend 7% of gross income – a budget that was confirmed by one PWC partner.

This benchmarking chapter is based on the IPA benchmarking surveys.

BENCHMARKING SOURCE ACKNOWLEDGEMENT AND COPYRIGHT

I gratefully acknowledge permission to use the IPA National Benchmarking as a basis for this chapter. The information above is all strictly the copyright of IPA. Please do not copy this or send in any format to any other accounting firm. PDF reports of each annual survey are normally available direct from Inside Public Accounting annually in November.

QUESTIONS TO ASK YOURSELF

1
Do you need to address the area of time on hours?

2
In what areas do the benchmarks assist you in clarifying your plans in the next 12 months?

3
In what areas do you need to create a policy or establish your future plans?

> ACCORDING TO **MIKE PLATT** OF IPA ABOUT **95 PER CENT** OF US FIRMS **STILL** COMES FROM THE '**DOLLARS** TIMES **HOURS**' FORMULA.

4 SNAKES OF COMPLACENCY

I was once told that I had three life choices: – to stand still, go forward or stand still. I subsequently decided that this was not sound counsel. I believe you either go forward or backward – to stand still is, by my definition, to go backward. Why? Because change is constant and if you stand still the world around you is moving forward. How easy is it to stand still in the world of accountancy? Many would say *"very easy"* and I would be inclined to agree.

One of my family members, for whom I acted personally, was the CEO of one of the UK's largest construction companies. His company turnover at the time was well over £1 billion. To say I was in admiration of him was an understatement, and I told him so. Interestingly, his response was to tell me how much he admired me – I had started a business - he had just kept one going for the founders of the construction company. That was a key point in changing my mental approach to my business. I decided I really wanted to grow a business and I also resolved that one day I wanted to create a company that had customers across the UK.

That was the motivator that helped me to avoid what I thought was small-minded thinking. I wished to avoid the snakes of complacency!

1   COMPLIANCE IS WHERE WE ARE AT

While I understand that there is less requirement for compliance services, the reality is that many firms still have 95 per cent of their work deriving from compliance. The challenge is to refuse to accept that you are just about compliance. What other business advisory or niche services can you add to your service portfolio? What other services do your clients require?

One of my seminar one liners is that we should do all we can to avoid the curse of mediocrity. In many ways this is a challenge to accounting firm owners – what will you do to transcend mediocrity?

2   UPDATE COMPLIANCE KNOWLEDGE

Sometimes firm owners admit that they are not up-to-date and rely on other partners or managers and sometimes comments are made in staff surveys that suggest that a partner is not on top of the technical side of life.

The observation I would make is that every firm owner should have one or more specialism(s) – and that may well include one or more of the compliance services. Combined there needs to be comprehensive compliance expertise across the owner group. If you are a sole owner – clearly that can be a challenge. You may well have a competent senior or long standing member of staff but it is always better to do all you can to keep up-to-date. Yes, I know that your job description says 'do it all' but the fact is that you may not be able to do just that. That is not an admission of failure – it is an honest assessment. Working excessive hours long term is not a satisfactory situation so work out what you have to do to make sure this business serves you and not vice versa. Your role and responsibility is to drive the business forward not for the business to drive you.

3 DOING A GOOD JOB AND DELIVERING BEST RESULTS

Commendable without question. And it may well be that you regard this as a satisfactory situation. But then, on the grounds that you are reading this, you may well be interested in achieving something different. You have a client base – what other service space could you occupy? How else can you serve clients? More importantly, what is your assessment of your future.

You might have low overhead costs and feel you are on a path that you are happy with and don't wish to engage with any of the other suggestions I have made thus far.

So, you should ensure that you ask all your clients to recommend you: *"Who else do you know that needs a really good accountant?"* Another strategy that might work is seeing which clients might wish to have periodic management accounts or which clients might be interested in bookkeeping services or payroll management.

4 MINIMUM CLIENT VISIBILITY

While you work behind your desk your clients don't see you and if all you ever do is complete the compliance work and your 'face time' with them is very little you will be vulnerable to losing those clients who perhaps want a more personal service, or better advice or maybe they might plan to take advantage of Cloud-based services.

The old maxim that 'people do business with people' is still true. But if this were updated it might say that people go where they receive the necessary service with the least effort.

Accountants normally see clients sometime between the hours of 8am to 6pm – do Cloud solutions enable clients to have this aspect of their responsibilities attended to outside of their work hours?

5   OWNERS DOING TOO MUCH ROUTINE WORK

Do you sometimes think you are doing too much of the routine work? So, you have tried delegation but still seem to end up with too much finishing off work. You have encouraged clients to do more of the routine work-balancing controls, verifying balances and so on.

The old maxim tells us that *"if you keep on doing what you've been doing you will keep on getting what you've been getting."* So, do you also need to assess your work-life balance? If you are doing more than 2800 total work hours a year the business is in control of you and not you in control of the business. Something has to change – and that change will probably include, (1) delegating some of the business administration, (2) making staff more accountable for finishing, or (3) if you do not have sufficiently trained staff and they have not responded to your needs then maybe finding new staff is your only option.

Someone once said to me, *"At some point in time the business needs to pay you back time as well as profit."* Wise counsel.

If you don't do something soon what will cause this imbalance to change?

6   NO TIME TO INNOVATE

Are you busy, busy, busy and have no quality time to sit, think and strategise? Then you are probably unable to spend time innovating.

Remember that your business is the firm's number one client – you need to prioritise investing time into your number one client and the owner(s).

7   EXPERIENCING PRICE ISSUES

Clients complaining about fees? Are you maybe thinking that you could not possibly increase fees?

The bottom line is:

When a client says, *"that's expensive"* it is important not to immediately go on the defensive. They are not complaining they are just making a comment. You could respond, *"Why do you think it is expensive?"*

Clients never leave because the fee is too high – they leave because the value is not high enough.

It is okay to lose clients who are not happy with the level of fees. There will always be more clients willing to engage you. It is in fact a healthy sign if you lose some clients as a result of the quantum of your fees.

Do you wish to build a business as a 'cheap' accountant? There will always be others (maybe working from home) who will promise to charge less.

Learn not to worry about this.

8   NO MARKETING INVESTMENT

In the chapter entitled 'Marketing' we discuss the quantum of the investment in marketing looking at time and spend.

Many think of the marketing spend as being about winning new clients – I don't. I have always believed that marketing is 80 per cent about marketing to clients and 20 per cent looking for new business.

Having won new clients it will be the quality of your service that keeps them as clients. But, you still need to be prepared to let clients have your technical help sheets, Budget Reports, Tax Cards and so on. Yes, they can also be used to win new clients.

Yes, many of your new clients come from satisfied clients. Long may they continue to do so.

So, marketing is not an optional management pursuit – it is an essential component of your firm's service to clients. It is a core component of your firm's value proposition.

And, yes, of course you will engage with your advocates and seek to bring in new business – new clients are the lifeblood of all professional businesses.

So, if you feel that you are predominately on a southerly facing ladder – what do you wish to do? What action? What results do you seek?

QUESTIONS TO ASK YOURSELF

What do you regard as your niche expertise?

Do you need to invest more time in enhancing your skillset?

How do you feel you can improve your timeliness of service?

> MOST **ACCOUNTANTS** DON'T **UNDERSTAND** THE DIFFERENCE BETWEEN GOOD **SERVICE** AND A REMARKABLE **EXPERIENCE**.
>
> ERIC GREGG

5 LADDERS OF SUCCESS

Firstly, let me state what I think is obvious and that is I am not presenting this as an all embracing list of what it takes for a firm to succeed. Allow me to at least state that I believe that the following covers at least 80 per cent of what it takes. Not sure you agree? Come with me on the journey that I have called the ladders of success.

1   NICHING

A term I learnt in North America where the locals there pronounce this 'nitching'. In the UK if the term is used it is pronounced neeche and never with the 'ing'. In fact the more common terminology is specialist services. So now you can probably identify which of your services fit into this category. It may help to look at the hierarchy of an accounting firm's service portfolio:

Compliance – normally comprising audit, accounts preparation and tax services. These may used as the foundation on which to build a portfolio of services that we looked at in the second chapter. But these services may not be what others call 'niche' services.

Niche services fall into two primary categories:

- Specialist [vertical] services by industry sector
- Specialist [lateral] services that can be delivered across your portfolio of clients

Services by industry sector could include manufacturing, car dealers, retail, technology, health care and so on. Services that can be delivered across your portfolio include payroll, management accounting, estate planning, IT hardware and software advice and so on.

The badges of niching include:

- Having a deep knowledge of the niche
- You probably have a personal brand attached to the niche
- You are probably devoting 300 or more hours a year to delivering services in the niche

- You will be able to speak knowledgeably on the niche to those in the sector
- You are able to write articles on the niche
- You have at least two case studies on your website involving the niche
- Your bio emphasises your specialism in this field
- You will have staff who also have specialist knowledge
- You will probably have clients outside your geographic area
- You will devote at least 100 hours or more a year to keeping up to date – in fact you are at the leading edge
- Finally, your niche interests you – in fact it may even excite you!

The benefits of being in a niche?

- There are fewer fish in the pond than for compliance services
- You are more likely to be able to establish a brand that is inextricably linked to the service
- You will be able to command higher fees
- You will have a group of dedicated advocates

For a range of niche services please refer to chapter 23.

2   UP SKILLING – PERSONAL AND I.T.

A firm and its team members must all have a commitment to personal development. Keeping up-to-date is taken for granted but here we are going beyond that and ensuring that we learn new skills.

What does it take to be at the leading edge?

What does it look like to inventory the new skills you could and should acquire?

What are others doing that you should be doing?

What is new on the horizon? When, in 2014 the ICAEW gained licensing rights for qualifying practitioners to deliver probate services one of my clients, a two-partner firm was one of the early adopters. Not only were they duly authorised to offer probate services but their marketing (brochure cards and newsletter) was in gear as was their networking.

What does your personal development plan look like in the next year? Two years?

How will you learn? Personal study. Courses. Webinars.

Who are the clients that you can serve? There is little point in developing a new service unless you have a clear strategy of identifying 'suspects' for your [new] service.

How does your development coincide with niching?

How can you broadcast the scope of your services so that you are occupying as much space in your clients lives as possible?

With both of these rungs on your success ladder how can you maximise the opportunities afforded by social media?

3 PRESENT AND FUTURE FOCUS

Imagine you are preparing for a seven day cycle challenge. Every day you plan to cycle 150 miles. You have never before cycled more than 30 miles in one day.

Planning a route would be a good place to start.

What else?

- Training
- Equipment
- Medical needs
- Spare bits and pieces
- A route

Yes, I have once or twice spent a week cycling so I know how painful it can be on the second day when you head for the bike and discover you are saddle sore.

Today, you (not me!) might want to tweet, blog and anything else that tells the world what a great time you are having.

In order to accomplish the mission you have to have a present and future focus. It is no different in an accounting business.

4 HIGH CLIENT VISIBILITY

Over the past decade or more we have become accustomed to judging our perception of service on the Internet by reference to such attributes as:

- Ease of navigation
- Price – many people automatically look at cost – but often don't order by reference to the lowest cost
- Reputation – what is the reputation or perhaps we should say 'performance' of the company?

Quality and being fit for purpose is taken for granted until…

So what does a firm need to achieve in order to be a success in this area?

The answer lies here and also in, 'Delivers value and on time'

It is understood that a website does not give a human personal experience – however online conversations and call backs can help to bridge that gap. The Cloud/Internet threat will inevitably mean that the veil or black tent or mystery surrounding professional services is removed. Few would engage an accountant unless they perceived it to be an absolute necessity so if they can have what they want using online technology what might happen to your fee income? The key, if there is one, is to embrace the technology AND to be personally available. That includes the main ways in which people communicate:

- Text
- Phone
- Email
- Social media
- Letters

And, in my view, most importantly being visible and meeting with clients one-on-one. The above list and visibility surely comprise the core components of services. The reality is that clients don't normally spend too long thinking about their accountant. So, in order to score a 10 out of 10 it is our responsibility to ensure we tick all the boxes of service.

5   GOOD AT DELEGATION

My first lesson in delegation came on the rugby field. One day the games teacher got fed up with me thinking that it was the right thing to do to just run with the ball – however I was no Jonah Lomu. *"Watch boy – you run with the ball"* while he passed the ball down the line and, of course, the pass down the three quarter line was quicker than my run.

Often we think, *"Only I can do it the right way"* or, *"Only I can do this,"* or, *"I can do it quicker myself,"* than maybe others you can think of.

In seminars when attendees are asked, *"How much of your work could you delegate?"* the range of responses indicate that somewhere between 10-20% of your work could well be delegated. This is work that maybe is going to take a chunk of time that you do not have right now, or work that needs some serious time set aside to research and consider. However, some of that work could also be good challenging work for others in your team. Yes, they might take longer than you but then their hourly [time] cost is less.

But as a firm owner you might have too much administration responsibility. Your professional training did not envisage you being an administration manager so as a business owner why not hire in a specialist to do this work? Or, at the very least find a trustworthy member of staff and extend their job description.

The fact is that prioritising time to see or contact clients is the most important 'to do' for an accountant. Meeting with your clients is your opportunity to explore how you can be of service.

What else you might need to do?

- Train staff
- Give them meaningful responsibility
- Listen to their ideas and take them seriously
- Give them feedback
- Ask them what you could do to make their role in this area more successful

Delegation idea – I delegated preparing the firm's accounts to one of my staff members.

6 INNOVATORS

We have probably heard of leading innovators such as Steve Jobs (Apple), James Dyson (Household appliances), Michelle Mone (Bras). Yet, all business people need to engage in innovation. Innovation starts with looking at something and believing it can be done better. That belief needs to be followed up by commitment, resources (time and money) and some sort of plan.

If we just start with the basics, innovation could look like:

- How can we improve our client engagement processes?
- How can we improve the processes for receiving client records?
- How do we speed up the preparation of accounts/tax returns?
- How can we improve client communications?
- How can we improve our standard letters to clients?
- How can we improve staff management?
- How can we be more effective with our marketing?
- How can we reduce our lock up?

I am sure you can create your own firm-specific list. Then for those that wish to move up a gear:

- How can we develop our online presence?
- How can we extend what we do via the Cloud?
- What new services should we commit to introducing?

What do you dream about (work wise)?

What solution could make that dream come about?

I conduct a number of staff surveys for accounting firms.

Here is a sample of feedback from staff on what innovations they would like:

> *"Quicker response times, perhaps by delegating more work down from manager levels."*
>
> *"Making sure a quick response is received by clients even if only a holding response."*

7   DELIVERS VALUE AND ON TIME

As with so many aspects of management there is often not just one answer, but delivering value is important or in my view absolutely essential. On the Internet a result is expected and value is anticipated. Likewise with professional services results and value are expected. Here is generically what I think most clients expect:

- Take my records and deliver the required end result
- Reassure me that I am not paying any more tax than is necessary
- Make sure I don't get caught with any interest or penalty costs
- Do the job as soon as I care to give you the records
- Impress me with your efficiency and firm-wide courtesy
- Bill me an amount that seems fair and reasonable

> **Key points:**
>
> Take what I have in the way of records and wave your magic wand. Then reassure me that I am paying the government the least amount and then don't surprise me with the quantum of your bill.

Some clients think: *"You want improvements to my records? You think I should change my accounting system? I will listen but there has to be a BIG reason and benefit for me – not just to reduce your time to keep your fee down."*

8   HAS A GOOD BRAND

A good brand is one that has attained prime space in your target customer's mind so that the brand is remembered as the customer's preferred solution. There are three overarching ingredients to creating a good brand. Getting these three ingredients working together is how you succeed in creating a good brand.

1   The right customer

To build a good brand, you need to focus on the best audience (target customer) for your brand. Determine your target customer values and focus your brand offering to that customer accordingly. This will mean sacrificing things valued by others and not by your target. Good branding requires sacrifice. You will fail if you try and be all things to all people.

2   A good brand promise, personality and position

If you don't lose sight of your target customer when you define your brand, then your chances of defining a good brand promise, personality and position are dramatically improved.

- A good brand promise combines fulfilling your customer's need with your team's passion.
- A good brand personality is authentic to your organisation, attractive to your target customer and consistently delivered.
- A good position is the clear reason your target customer will fulfill their need with your promise instead of a competitive solution.

3   Great commitment by your team

The branding journey begins with targeting the right customer and developing a good brand strategy, but it does not end there. A good brand delivers a consistent experience from initial brand awareness right through the entire customer experience – sales, delivery, solution experience, billing and any after-care or support. To get all aspects of your operations (as opposed to only your marketing campaigns) on brand, you need to ensure you have a strong commitment from your team. Having an A+ commitment from your team is a vital (but often overlooked) ingredient to good branding.

CHARACTERISTICS OF HIGH GROWTH FIRMS

Inside Public Accounting reports that Hinge, a US based marketing and branding company analysed responses from 526 high-growth professional service firms. This included over 120 accounting firms with an average annual growth rate of at least 20 per cent. Hinge partner Sylvia Montgomery says that these firms are different because of their business development approach, unique culture, entrepreneurial business model, use of the latest technology and highly experienced and specialised staff.

Results from the Hinge study also revealed that 75 per cent of high growth firms are more likely to be specialised and put 23 per cent less effort (money and time) into traditional services and a 13 per cent greater investment into digital marketing than no-growth firms.

PS – A FIRM THAT COMMITS TO INVESTING IN THE FUTURE

The accountancy profession does not have a reputation for being at the leading edge of innovation. But as noted above – there are plenty of opportunities to innovate.

Many accountants I know do not have a business plan as such – their definition of a business plan is at best a budget!

QUESTIONS TO ASK YOURSELF

1
How much of your revenues currently emanate from compliance?

2
What do you need to do to take a giant leap away from being complacent? What do you need to take a step forward to being more successful?

3
Which of the eight 'rungs' do you plan to address?

> UNLESS **COMMITMENT** IS MADE, THERE ARE **ONLY PROMISES** AND **HOPES**; BUT NO **PLANS**.
>
> PETER F. DRUCKER

6 STRATEGIC PLANNING

Before we leave the introductory chapters of Foundations I would like to record a few thoughts with regard to the importance of crystallising your plans into a strategic plan. In short, strategic planning is a process, the result of which is a written document that sets forth where an organisation wants to go and how it will get there. Some suggest that an accounting firm's strategic plan should consider a five-year horizon. It should envisage how big the firm aims to become, where it will have office locations, what its major service expertise will be and what the client base will look like.

Once the firm's owners reach consensus on these big picture issues, the firm can develop its one year and three year goals and objectives and then determine the strategies and tactics to achieve them. Strategies and tactics are more short term in nature. They should be specific, achievable and measureable within a year.

Strategic planning looks at the future, while many, if not most, accounting firms have a very short-term view of the world. Reward systems often revolve around the billable hour with little reward for non-billable time invested in the firm's future. That's very dangerous – short sighted to say the least.

KEYS TO SUCCESSFUL STRATEGIC PLANNING

Establish a sense of urgency

A sufficient number of accountants in the firm must believe that it is no longer business as usual and that strategic direction is necessary if the firm is to maximise its potential and the owner's aspirations. They must instil and constantly reinforce a sense of urgency that change is necessary.

Firm leadership must have a genuine commitment to develop and implement a strategic plan. Without strong leadership and passionate commitment, it is still 'business as usual,' despite the rhetoric. Under these circumstances, the firm's efforts will never be at their optimum.

Involve all firm owners in the process

The owners need to buy in and support the plan. By involving each of them in the process through a series of one-on-one meetings and/or a group brainstorming session each owner will identify with the process. Ownership is really important.

Key managers also need to buy into the future of the firm and be excited by the path ahead. Special programmes that enlist their support will add to the plan's successful implementation.

Keep the plan simple and focused

If the firm is developing its first strategic plan, it should keep it simple and focused. Most firms try to take on too much, too fast and end up accomplishing little. In fact belief and credibility may suffer.

I am often asked for a checklist on what has to be done to create a strategic plan so here are some outline thoughts.

Key points in strategic planning:

1. Keep it simple – it is important to use an uncomplicated process that is results-oriented
2. Don't start planning until you have a solid commitment from the leadership
3. Ensure that your key executives are active participants in the process
4. Expect and train each team member to look at the interests of the entire company
5. Keep the size of the group small (5-10)
6. Don't have the Managing Partner or a key manager run the strategy sessions. Instead select a trained facilitator who will pay attention to agenda, procedures and keeping the discussion on track
7. Don't seek perfection. Aim for the best plan you can in the time you have available and then make sure there is a total commitment to implementation
8. Break the process up into separate sessions of a few days, over maybe a month or two. But be sure to have a timetable and keep up the momentum
9. Pay close attention to assumptions. Test and challenge
10. Be cautious and be prepared to say 'no' to some opportunities
11. Build into the plan procedures for monitoring progress on the plan and for assessing results.

CORE COMPONENTS OF AN EFFECTIVE STRATEGIC PLAN

Where are we today?

An environmental review

External environment

- The economy – how is this impacting your clients and prospects?
- The markets and sectors you wish to be in
- The clients you wish to act for
- Your competitors – what are they offering? What is their pricing strategy?
- Impact of technology on people's behaviour

Internal environment

- Financial position – Capex. Lock up. Profitability
- Organisational structure – Equity. Non equity. Departmental.
- Growth trends – what is historical. What is achievable. Realistic
- Pricing position
- Capacity. What does stretch look like? Improving timeliness.

Analysis of strengths, weaknesses, (both internal) threats and opportunities (both external)

Drilling down into specifics – ensuring that they are all joined up

Marketing, Sales, Production, Innovation, Finances, Administration, Human Resources.

Where do we wish to go?

What should we assume?

- Economic growth
- Compliance services - growing, stable or in decline
- Competitors – those in geographic proximity. Cloud based
- Technology – what investment is required. Training
- Access to funding
- Access to talent

A Mission Statement is important

- Begin with the end in mind
- Ensure it is compelling and inspiring

- Focuses on the benefits your people derive from the organisation
- Eliminates conflict and channel resources
- Are not goals; but about the on-going direction
- Is not financial
- Is not focussed on quality of service
- Not carved in stone, but also not changed on a whim

HOW DO WE GET THERE?

Identify Key Result areas

Establish goals by Key Result area

Establish SMART goals

> **S**pecific
>
> **M**easurable
>
> **A**chievable
>
> **R**ealistic
>
> **T**ime based (or could be trackable)

What are the hot prospects?

Existing clients – cross serving opportunities. What are client needs? Where can we occupy more space?

Prospective clients – who are the suspects? Who are our prospects - by service –by industry? By definition – family owned, entrepreneurial. Growth. Not for profit etc.

Marketing

- What needs to be continued? Discontinued?
- Investment. Time. Money
- Targets. Tracking. Accountability.
- Options. Technology. Social media. Paper based. PR. Other routes to prospects?
- Fee potential – From existing clients. From new clients?

An effective strategic planning process should plan to:

- Improve growth and profitability
- Reveal hidden pitfalls and risks

- Help you deal with future uncertainty
- Help you become more opportunity-oriented
- Provide common understanding and coordination of effort
- Provide a means to reach and revise agreement
- Build motivation, enthusiasm, unity of purpose, and commitment through involved participation
- Boost morale because the participants belong to an organisation that knows where it is going
- Relieve anxieties by making known the previously unknown or the 'hard to address' and dealing with it
- Help you reach and stretch for higher levels of attainment
- Provide a coordinated business plan which stakeholders will find attractive
- Build a stronger competitive position

QUESTIONS TO ASK YOURSELF

Do you have a Strategic Plan – if not will you commit to creating one?

Do you have a Business Plan – if not will you commit to creating one?

What are your own medium term and long term objectives and milestones?

> **DO NOT ALLOW PAST MISTAKES TO SHAPE YOUR FUTURE.**
>
> LORNA JACKIE WILSON

DRIVING YOUR PROFITS UP

7 FIRM AND PARTNER PERFORMANCE MODEL

I was first introduced to the Partner Performance model by Dave Cottle (my co-author of Clients 4Life) who had first seen this when studying the Weiner Worksheet, developed by Ron Weiner of New York. The model was developed by David Maister. I find this provides valuable insight into the core model of how you can look at an accounting firm and the keys to how you can take management decisions that improve firm profitability. So often management material is adopted by many and I wish to give credit where it is due.

THE FOUR TYPES OF MANAGEMENT ACTIVITY

Our firm revenues are derived from our productivity (doing the work) and our pricing (the amount we charge).

Our net income is the revenue, less the cost of earning that revenue (cost management), less the write downs taken (client management).

Therefore, in generating a profit firms engage in four types of management activity:

1. Productivity
2. Pricing
3. Cost management
4. Client management

These four management activities combine and provide five keys that influence the quantum of the bottom line.

THE FIVE KEYS TO FIRM PROFITABILITY

Long term keys:

1. Leverage (L)
2. Margin (M)

Short term keys:

3. Billing rate (B)
4. Utilisation (U)
5. Realisation (R)

DEFINING THESE TERMS

Leverage (L)

Leverage is the total number of professional and support people in the firm divided by the number of firm owners.

> **Example:** a firm with 9 owners and 19 professional and support staff has a total of 28 personnel and a leverage of 3.1 Thus an owner has responsibility for managing himself and three staff members.

Margin (M)

Margin is the economic net profit percentage on net fees.

$$\text{Margin} = \frac{\text{Economic net profit on net fees}}{\text{Net fees}}$$

Billing rate (B)

The firm billing rate is the weighted average standard billing rate per hour. It is calculated by dividing the standard fees – the total billing at standard rates – by the total chargeable hours.

$$\text{Billing rate} = \frac{\text{Standard fees}}{\text{Total chargeable hours}}$$

Utlisation (U)

Utilisation is the average annual chargeable hours per person.

> **Example:** In the last twelve months –
> Total chargeable hours   38,910
> Total personnel   28
> Utilisation   =   1,390

Realisation (R)

Realisation is the net fees billed (after write downs and write ups) expressed as a percentage of standard fees.

> **Example:** An engagement with a standard fee of £10,000 is billed for £9,000. Realisation is £9,000 divided into £10,000 = 90%

FIRM CASE STUDY

	Firm 1	Firm 2	Firm 3	Firm 4
Partners	8	9	6	8
Total personnel	64	28	106	60
Leverage (L)	8.0	3.1	17.7	7.5
Chargeable hours	65,728	38,910	109,866	89,946
Utilisation (U)	1,027	1,390	1,036	1,499
Standard fees	8,216,000	3,945,500	15,910,352	9,857,084
Billing rate per hour (B)	125	101	145	110
Net fees (the top line)	6,983,600	3,870,535*	11,932,764	9,817,655
Realisation % (R)	85.0%	98.1%	75.0%	99.6%
Net Income (the bottom line)	2,095,080	1,327,593	2,756,468	3,642,350
Margin % (M)	30.0%	34.3%	23.1%	37.1%
Net Income Per Partner (NIPP)	261,885	147,510	459,411	455,294

*__Key point:__ The net billing rate per hour is 106.25. What is yours?

It is interesting to note that net income per partner can be calculated as follows:

$$L \times U \times B \times R \times M = NIPP$$

e.g.   8 x 1027 x 125 x 85% x 30% = 261,855

The short-term keys provide the immediate opportunity to increase the firm's profitability. Let us look at some examples.

WHAT IS THE BOTTOM LINE EFFECT FOR FIRM 1 OF:

An increase in utilisation: Hours

Currently   1,027

Increase to   1,077

An increase of   50

Revenue increase of (64 x 50) hours = 3,200 hours @ 125 = 400,000 @ 85% = 340,000

Increase in NIPP = 42,500 (16.2%)

An increase in the hourly billing rate

Billing rate at present   125

Increase to   126

Increase of   1

Total increase of 1 for all hours, assuming all realised = 65,728

Increase in NIPP = 8,216 (3%)

An increase in realisation: %

Realisation at present   85.00

Increase to   86.00

Increase of   1.0

Revenue increase of 1% of 8,216,000 assuming all realised = 82,160

Increase in NIPP of – 10,270 (3.9%)

SOME STRATEGIES FOR IMPROVING YOUR SHORT TERM KEYS

Let us look at what I call the TUBR model. This is the personalised version of the LUBRM model and looks like this:

PARTNER CASE STUDY

		Partner 1	Partner 2	Partner 3	Partner 4
Total hours	T	2,400	2,400	2,400	2,400
Utilised percentage	U	50%	35%	60%	60%
Client chargeable		1,200	840	1,440	1,440
Billing rate	B	160	140	250	200
Standard time		192,000	117,600	360,000	288,000
Realisation	R	85%	75%	85%	65%
Net fees		163,200	88,200	306,000	187,200
Variance (1 and 2 and 3 and 4)			75,000		118,800
Variance %			46%		39%
Variance (2 and 3)				217,800	
Variance %				247%	

The only new key is the 'T' which is for total hours. Study the variables and note that when comparing partners 1 and 2, partner 1 is making a contribution of 75,000 more as a result of higher chargeable hours (360); higher charge rate (by 14%), and a higher realisation (by 10%).

Similarly if we compare partners 3 and 4, partner 3 is making 118,800 more than partner 4 from the same number of hours. The table above reveals that this is achieved through a higher charge rate and a higher realisation rate.

Now compare partners 2 and 3. Higher chargeable hours, charge rate and realisation give an increase in profit of almost 250% with profit of 306,000 compared to 88,200.

Extreme example? Not at all, I can assure you there are greater extremes than shown in this case study.

1. Utilisation

	STRATEGY	ALREADY DONE	CONSIDER	TO ACTION
1	Set yourself a chargeable hours target for the year			
2	Capture your time daily. Those owners who capture time daily report an increase in chargeable hours of between 4-6%			
3	Use the '50 minute hour'			
4	Consider using the '15 minute hour.' This is where you give advice that you have specifically researched for another client and you wish the time records to reflect that time which is not necessary to be spent researching again.			
5	Seek to reduce or eliminate any areas or practices that cause you not to charge time. For example, if there is a strong firm culture on high realisation, you may conclude that it would be wiser to avoid some of this pressure by not recording all the hours worked			
6	Develop a structured programme for meeting your clients			
7	Monitor your utilisation regularly			
8	Don't 'donate' time to clients			
9	Review your job scheduling process and determine if it can be improved			

2. Realisation

STRATEGY		ALREADY DONE	CONSIDER	TO ACTION
1	Bill more promptly, while the tears of appreciation are still moist in client's eyes			
2	Send interim bills			
3	Ensure that problems encountered on field work are raised with the client immediately. In this instance the interaction with the client establishes who assumes responsibility for solving the problem and how much this will cost above the 'normal' fee if it is agreed that your firm is responsible for solving the problem			
4	Be careful with fixed fees unless you are sure that you will generate at least the required realisation rate			
5	Don't schedule assignments wall-to-wall. Allow time for the person in charge of the engagement to complete the work so that the bill can be raised without delay	✓		
6	If you have a situation where you are likely to realise less than 85% of standard consider asking other [co-owners] for their advice on the quantum of the account			

	STRATEGY	ALREADY DONE	CONSIDER	TO ACTION
7	Who is responsible for billing your jobs? It is possible that the engagement manager may have a better knowledge of the work input. Delegating billing to managers normally results in higher realisation. Managers may be future firm owners – allow them the opportunity to practice and hone their billing skills			
8	Reduce price sensitivity by exceeding clients' expectations. Look at what is provided from the client's perspective. The client assumes technical expertise; he or she expects, and is entitled to, more than that			
9	Beware of the anchor of last years' bill			

3. Billing Rate

	STRATEGY	ALREADY DONE	CONSIDER	TO ACTION
1	Consider raising your personal charge rate by two times the rate of inflation. This increases the value of 'time on', not the amount you bill the client			
2	Introduce a higher charge rate where higher value work is undertaken. A premium for work that has greater value is a generally accepted principle			
3	Consider raising fees on your most aggravating clients. If you lose them as a result, you may be better off			

4	Who are your worst clients? Who do staff think are your worst clients? Consider 'firing' the worst clients thus freeing up more time with the best clients			
5	When concerns are raised about the quality of service provided, don't compromise on fees – aim to provide an enhanced service instead			
6	Select clients carefully – some clients will always complain about fees and you don't need this type of client. Even clients with potential for high fees may not be worth it in the long run			

A FEW MORE GENERAL POINTS THAT RELATE TO IMPROVING MARGIN

Make sure that so far as possible you delegate down so that you do not undertake work that could be completed by junior staff

- Keep investing in training and feedback as this will enable you to improve your future leverage – this is a key strategy for building value
- Do all you can to help junior staff gain clients' confidence
- How can you make better use of non chargeable time? Make sure that no one is just writing off time. Non chargeable time is firm investment time

TIME: AN INVESTMENT AND ONE OF YOUR RAW MATERIALS

Investment definition: 'To lay out with an expectation of gain'.

1. Client investment time – both you and the client are looking for a return
2. Firm investment time – CPD, holidays, marketing and so on

I find it interesting that the range of chargeable and total hours for firm owners varies greatly. Allow me to illustrate my point by reviewing a few areas. In looking at some of these key performance indicators I recognise I am addressing my peers, who in some cases have enjoyed a longer career than my 16 years as an accounting firm owner. However I have spent many years consulting with accounting firms and these insights are gleaned from my experiences both as a practitioner and consultant. My knowledge has been enhanced by other consultants and books written by many distinguished authors. The purpose of this training programme is not to produce a book like Clients 4Life with its 400 pages, but to look at a number of key areas that, to some extent, revolve around the TUBR and LUBRM models. We will look at other areas of performance and owner input in the forthcoming chapters.

TIME ON: WHAT IS YOUR FIRM INPUT?

When I started as a trainee accountant it seemed that jobs lasted for either one week or a multiple of weeks. While that was many years ago, I was interested to find that my youngest son, decades later while training to become a Chartered Accountant had his time occupied with audits that last one week, two weeks or three. In that situation completing a time sheet with 37½ hours is easy because it is all chargeable to one client. Moving the clock forward to when I became a manager I recall that at the end of the week my time sheet had some full days at clients and others when my time sheet had time charged to two or three clients. Roll the clock forward to when I was a firm owner and there were times when I struggled to account for five hours, let alone seven and a half. My daily time sheet might have 20 client entries, but some were for only 10 minutes.

So, what does the 'time on' scene look like today? Let's start by looking at some 'facts'.

Firm owners' time is not normally confined to 9-5. Many practitioners work more than 40 hours a week, even though not evidenced by their time sheet. Consider:

1. You may not be fully recording your client time
2. You may find the prospect of your time recording demotivating
3. Surveys show that when total time is captured total hours vary from 2,200-2,800 hours per annum, per owner, with an average of 2,450
4. Inter firm surveys show that owner chargeable hours per annum vary from 600 to 1,350 hours with an average of 1,000 per owner
5. By deduction some partners have 'non chargeable' time in excess of their chargeable time.

INVESTING YOUR TIME

As a firm owner you undoubtedly expect to earn more than when you were a manager. In return for a greater income there are a number of requirements for firm owners. One of these is the time invested *in* and *on* the business. The benchmark I have evidenced time and time again is that a 'well managed' firm normally has partner/owner investment in the region of 2,400 hours per annum.

You may well be close to that already. If you work on average a nine hour day (maybe allowing 30 minutes for lunch) then that represents a 45 hour week and a 2,340 hour year. That also means your holidays are recorded at 9 hours for each day and similarly with sickness, CPD and so on.

Inter firm surveys in the 1980s both in the UK and US showed that the average firm owner time on and chargeable to clients was in the region of 1200. Now time on for firm owners in the US (as evidenced by surveys undertaken by IPA) indicate somewhere in the region of 1150 chargeable hours while in the UK many partners fail to raise their time on over 1000 with many delivering less than 900.

How many total hours are you investing in the firm? Does this need to increase? Alternatively, does there need to be a decrease? Quality of life is important and while a temporary increase over 2800 hours a year might sometimes be necessary it is essential that you manage your time commitment with the firm to ensure it does not 'steal' your life away from all the other components of life such as family, rest, health and other interests or responsibilities.

We will be looking at your time on and in particular your client 'visible' time and your marketing *investment* comprised in your firm time.

Your time 'dustbin' and downtime

If you commit to capturing all your time, it is inevitable that there will be time that you cannot account for. Beware the trap of 'admin' or whatever other dustbin you are accustomed to writing up your time to. Use a downtime cost centre to capture this time - at least for the partners.

FIRM OWNER BOTTOM LINE SURVEY

Owners are required to be effective in managing in the following areas:

	ON A SCALE OF 1-10 HOW DO YOU RATE YOUR PERFORMANCE	TARGET	GAP
1. Achieving chargeable and total (investment) hours			
2. Maximising visibility with clients			
3. Maintaining and enhancing personal capabilities			
4. Achieving target for client meetings			
5. Engaging with professional referrals			
6. Winning new clients			
7. Maximising service opportunities with existing clients			
8. Minimising the lock up %			
9. Maximising the realisation %			
10. Transferring your skills to other firm owners and staff			
11. Bringing in work for other people to work on			
12. Bringing in new work from which the team can learn new skills			

QUESTIONS TO ASK YOURSELF

1
Does utilisation need to increase? If so, what needs to happen?

2
What is your target for your net hourly billing rate?

3
Do you have a second [higher than standard] billing rate?

> LET OUR **ADVANCE** WORRYING BECOME ADVANCE **THINKING** AND **PLANNING**.
>
> **WINSTON CHURCHILL**

8 YOUR **PERSONAL DEVELOPMENT** AND SKILL **ENHANCEMENT**

> **Question 1:** What have you learned in the last year to make yourself more valuable to your clients?

> **Question 2:** What will you learn in the next year to make yourself more valuable to your clients?

> **Question 3:** As you develop your skills what is going to be your special claim to fame?

What is your personal development plan? If there were a ladder inside your brain, would you still be on the same rung as last year looking at the same views, or would you have climbed higher and be looking at new and more interesting vistas?

What have you learned in the last year that has heightened your skills and knowledge and made you more valuable to your clients?

YOUR CORE COMPETENCY – STILL UP-TO-DATE?

No doubt you attend all the courses and read all the press releases and technical updates that ensure you are up-to-date. However, with ever-increasing legislation, regulation and technology there can be a time when keeping up-to-date is not top of your agenda, or maybe even on the list. This applies especially if you have others around who are not co-owners and whose job responsibility it is to be up-to-date. When you look ahead at the remainder of your career, what services and advice would you like to offer? What opportunities might you have?

Some practitioners, especially those who are sole owners, are required to keep abreast in most general practice areas but then outsource engagements where specialist advice is required. They keep an eye on change and make it their business to be in the know. Some practitioners have specialised either in an industry or a particular service. How do you wish to extend your own knowledge? What can you learn and then practice?

REVITALISING YOUR NEW PERSONAL DEVELOPMENT REGIME PAYS DIVIDENDS

As knowledge workers we have a virtually unlimited capacity to learn and the opportunity to engage clients who want and need that expertise. The analogy with following a physical fitness regime provides a parallel. It takes commitment to studying and not to be deterred or give up. If you have started but your commitment has waned, resolve to resume.

As you enhance your knowledge this will help you develop your Unique Advisory Skills (UAS). The quality and incisiveness of your advice maintains your position as a valued adviser, especially with those B clients for whom you wish to deliver more visible time and who have previously viewed your service as more product than service.

Competition among accountants is intense and with clients unable to easily compare one firm's tax or accounts service with another, your UAS can be an important factor in the decision as to which firm to appoint as accountant. Your firm's UAS is certainly prominent in client retention and satisfaction.

Technology has further empowered governmental and regulatory organisations to prescribe the formats in which we submit returns. Uniformity it seems is now obligatory, but the drive for uniformity has resulted in reports, forms, formats and procedures that are not always easy for clients to understand or follow.

BEYOND COMPLIANCE

Technical CPD maintains your expertise up-to-date. Further, advanced study and delivery of assignments in the area of your compliance skills may well elevate you to the status of a specialist – within the firm and possibly even in the community.

But, if high level expertise is not your vocation – what will you specialise in? You probably know little [and care even less] about how a modern car engine works (I don't now and yet once upon a time I was able to de-coke a car engine). Similarly, clients care little about your level of compliance expertise. Going back to the car engine analogy – you don't care how the car engine works so long as it fires into life when the ignition system is activated. In the same way clients assume you are technically competent in respects of matters appertaining to compliance – unless they discover otherwise.

I recommend that in order to develop a high level of expertise there needs to be a combination of varying types of education/experience. But before we list these there are two absolutely fundamental requirements to succeed outside the compliance boundaries:

1. An inner resolve and passion to extend your personal service capabilities in the area of your chosen specialisation. You will need

this to keep the flame burning brightly when maybe the work you would like to do is not as readily available as you would like.
2. The prospect of there being [some] work in this field of expertise that will over time provide the challenge you expect as well as the return in the form of fees.

The development of your skill set in your chosen field, as well as depending on the likelihood of you being able to deliver value to clients includes all or some of the following:

1. Structured learning – courses or study
2. Experience – learning through osmosis
3. An office support team
4. A network of other professionals
5. A marketing and sales strategy
6. A clear value proposition.

RECOMMENDED READING LIST

Please visit the downloads section of my website (www.marklloydbottom.com) and download my Recommended Reading Lists.

QUESTIONS TO ASK YOURSELF

1
What new skills will you commit to developing?

2
What are you famous for?

3
What value does that add to the bottom line?
Should this be greater?

IT IS **NOT** THE **STRONGEST** SPECIES THAT **SURVIVE**, **NOR** THE MOST **INTELLIGENT**, BUT THE **ONES** WHO ARE MOST **RESPONSIVE** TO **CHANGE**.

CHARLES DARWIN

9 THE **COST** OF **POOR** SERVICE AND THE **POTENTIAL** VALUE OF **OUSTANDING** CLIENT **SERVICE**

What is the financial cost of lost clients? If you had not lost some of those clients, where would you be today? Now, I realise this is a hypothetical question and I also think that you may be thinking that you are better off without some of those clients that once adorned your client list. What about those clients who went elsewhere without you ever really knowing why? Or those clients who cited the level of your fees as the reason for leaving? Most consultants to the accounting profession know that the real reason why clients leave is not because of the level of fees but the inadequate level of service.

> **Key Point:** Clients don't leave because your fees are too high, they leave because the value is not high enough.

Let us imagine at this stage that your clients might spend more with you than just paying for compliance work. We will examine this in greater depth in the subsequent session. What additional revenue earning opportunities might be available to you? My book Clients 4Life sets out what needs to be done to deliver outstanding service so that your clients not only remain with you, they recommend you and come back for more services. This book seeks to encourage you to advance a number of ways in which you can yourself go on a journey of improving service levels in your firm. To start with I would like you to calculate the cost of lost clients using the formula set out below. I first came across this when working with Practice Management Consultant, August Aquila and have since developed this to calculate the value of being a firm that is committed to delivering outstanding service.

Let's start by calculating the cost of lost clients using the following table:

		YOUR FIRM	EXAMPLE
1	Enter the number of existing clients		100
2	Enter the number of clients you lose each year		10

THE COST OF POOR SERVICE AND THE POTENTIAL OF OUTSTANDING CLIENT SERVICE | 9

3	Multiply the number of clients who leave each year (my example is 50%) by the percentage of clients citing poor service as the reason		5
4	Enter the average gross profit per client		500
5	Multiply the average gross profit (No.4) per client by the number of clients leaving due to poor service (No.3)		2,500
6	Enter the cost to attract a new client		500
7	Multiply the cost to attract a new client (No.6) by the number of clients lost to poor service (No.3)		2,500
8	Add lost gross profit (No.5) to cost to attract a new client (No.7)		5,000
9	Enter the answer to No.8 here – this is the annual cost of poor service to your firm		5,000

COST OF CLIENTS LOST THROUGH ATTRITION

But what about calculating the cost of clients lost through natural attrition? Clients may move to another area, cease to be in business, retire or die. These clients also have to be replaced if the firm is to grow.

10	Clients lost through attrition (No.2-No.3)		5
11	Multiply No.10 x No.4 (gross profit per client)		2,500
12	Add No.9 to No.11 to value annual client loss		7,500

Having identified the annual cost of lost clients, it is important to recognise that this is an annual loss. It is often accepted that the average lifetime of a client is seven years so in order to calculate the lifetime cost, the annual cost should be multiplied by 7, or any other number you may deem more appropriate.

13	Multiply No.12 by No.7 to give a seven year 'lifetime' cost		52,500

The financial gain of outstanding client service

If you were to review your analysis of fees raised in the last year, what specific level of fees would be attributable to non-compliance work? Then separate out the non-compliance fees where the client either asked you for service or their circumstances dictated that they needed your other services. The remaining revenue is likely to represent services that have been sold to the client on merit. Now, if you are to be the client's trusted advisor my question is how much additional revenue can you generate from your 'extension' services? That is, all those other services that you have to offer that do not fall under the banner of being a compliance service?

I am going to ask you to stretch your thinking. For the purposes of this next calculation I am going to lower the bar considerably so that we enter the nitty gritty world of reality as opposed to [very valid] theory. What extra services do you think you could deliver? As I don't wish to make this calculation overly complicated I am going to ask you to enter your annual gross profit and then select a percentage between 15 and 25.

1	Enter the firm's gross profit		200,000
2	Multiply No.1 by 15%		30,000
3	Multiply No.2 by 25%		50,000
4	Select a number between the answer for No.2 and No.3, or lower if this reflects your view, to reflect your view of the potential gross profit you can achieve from delivering extension services to clients		40,000

This 'credit' comes through having a range of extension services to offer clients. Yes, that means going beyond compliance work but this offers the opportunity to deliver something of greater value that will help your clients with their future planning and success. Again, multiply the annual gain by 7 unless you have a good reason to select another multiplier.

5	Multiply No.4 x 7 to give a seven year 'lifetime' gain		280,000

BRINGING IT ALL TOGETHER

In the first part of the calculation we focused on the lifetime cost of clients lost through poor service combined with the cost of the loss through attrition. Let us regard this as the debit of lost business. In 5 above you identified the potential credit through your range of non-compliance services.

Now calculate the 7 year result of delivering outstanding client service by:

6	Adding the lifetime cost (No.13) to the lifetime gain (No. 5) give the management value range of delivering outstanding client service		332,500

QUESTIONS TO ASK YOURSELF

1

Where does your service need to improve?

2

What additional profit will ensue?

3

How much potential revenue can you target to achieve from delivering outstanding client service?

> EVEN THE **BEST** COMPANIES HAVE **SERVICE** ISSUES. IT'S NOT THAT YOU **MESSED** UP, BUT HOW YOU **HANDLE** IT THAT **COUNTS**.
>
> LEISA GILL, CHIEF EXPERIENCE LEADER, LBMC

10 CLIENT MEETINGS

WHAT ARE CLIENTS' NEEDS?

Suppose there were no regulatory obligations to promote demand for your services. Just for one earth shattering moment, assume the taxation authorities devised a tax system that requires no submission of financial statements with all taxes received based on some other criteria such as a triennial assessment or sales tax.

And let's further assume there is no regulatory requirement to have or file audited accounts and the personal tax filing is so easy that everyone files online using their digital tax account.

The point to consider is what the effect would be if there was no compliance work. Setting aside the impact on the number of firms and so on, one certain outcome is that you would focus 100 per cent on meeting the wants of clients. There would be no compelling reason to hire an accountant and so services would be based on want and value as determined by the client and not on needs demanded by regulation.

> **Key point:** Surveys inform us that the businessperson regards their accountant as their number one business adviser – an accolade rarely applied to the business consultant, the bank manager, the insurance adviser, members of the family or team members.

Does this accord with your own understanding of how clients view your role?

Well, it depends on which clients we're talking about. Most practitioners have higher value or A clients, clients who demand your time and are happy to pay your fees. Let's assume these are business clients and about five per cent of your clients.

That leaves 95 per cent of your business client list. Among these there are clients who will never engage you for any service other than the most basic of compliance service. Some of them seek a product service, and most likely cost is a major factor in the decision regarding who to hire. No matter what you do to interest them in looking at planning opportunities, you know you and your firm will rarely be on their radar screen, other than when absolutely necessary.

What percentage of your clients do you place in this category? Please, be careful at this juncture not to make too many assumptions and write off too many of your clients, as Double Your Income is designed to challenge those assumptions! So, how many of your clients do you think would engage you for one of your other services? Maybe some business owners do not take the role of adviser or facilitator seriously, but how many?

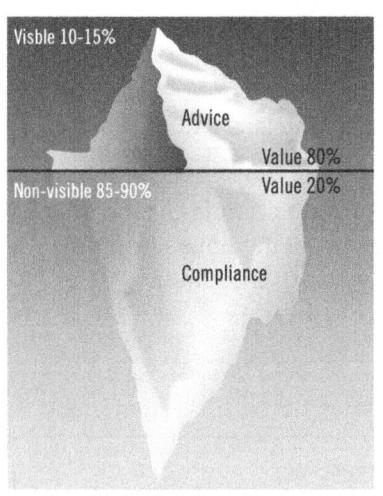

THE ICEBERG OF TIME

As the captain and passengers on the Titanic found, 85-90 per cent of the mass of an iceberg lies hidden beneath the ocean's surface. It's not visible, but that critical mass exists and supports the visible 10-15 per cent.

Similarly, as accountants much of the time we spend is not visible to the client. The client knows we need their records and at some point in time their financial statements or tax returns will be completed. Based on our research we can now attach a number to those visible hours, with the typical client being face-to-face with the accountant for somewhere in the region of 150 minutes during a 12 month period.

The mass of the invisible iceberg has a major role to play to support the visible top of the iceberg. But unlike the iceberg whose mass beneath the surface is relatively constant, the iceberg's value principle serves to demonstrate the value of increasing that which is visible.

THE ICEBERG'S VALUE PRINCIPLE

> **Key point:** 80 per cent of what clients value takes place in the personal interactions between the client and the partner. These are the 'magical' moments.

Question: And so, the remainder of the 80 per cent of the time you spend doesn't have any value?

Answer: No, that's not what I mean. The iceberg's value principle shows us clients place a strong emphasis on the importance of the visible relationship. It's the one-on-one meetings when they hear good advice and sound judgment.

THE ICEBERG'S VALUE PROPOSITION

Key Assumption: Let's take an example whereby you spend two hours with a client over a twelve month period and then assume the value of these meetings, as perceived by the client, is 80 per cent of the total service delivered. If you could increase this time from two to four hours...would the value increase to 160 per cent? Considering the extra two hours might be spent on profitability enhancement, management problem solving, client centric or other future-focused services, it should have great value. While mathematically we should adjust the percentages so they total 100 per cent, we do not suggest that the value of the invisible, compliance related work has any less value.

> **Key point:** Thus, the iceberg of time's value proposition is that adding only a small number of additional client facing hours into the client relationship massively increases the value to the client.

THE REAR VIEW MIRROR PERSPECTIVE

The accountants view

Our work has, for the most part, an historical perspective.

The client's view

How does a business owner spend their time? Like the accountant, business owners occupy themselves with plying their trade including buying, selling, producing, marketing, managing, and making decisions. In doing so, the business owner focuses on the present and future. Yesterday is history. The hotel owner cannot sell rooms that were vacant the previous night; he or she can only sell rooms that remain unsold today. The businessperson pays heed to yesterday when paying bills, chasing payments, dealing with service problems...and when the accountant calls.

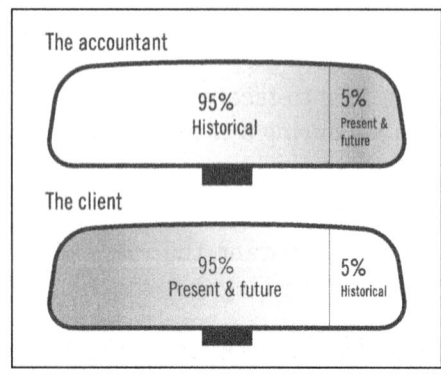

How much time do your clients' spend on historical matters? We obviously don't know the answer precisely, but five per cent may not be too wide of the mark.

HOW AND WITH WHO DO YOU SPEND YOUR TIME?

How you spend your time is a major component of your client service value equation. With 8,760 hours in a year, an owner-accountant typically spends 2,200-2,400 hours working. Of these, it is usual for between 800-1,200 hours to be chargeable. Interestingly, time recording systems do not routinely permit an analysis of the time you spend face-to-face with clients (visible time) as opposed to other time, which we call desktop time, or non-visible time.

THE JAW-DROPPING CASE OF THE DENTIST'S RECEPTIONIST

Fellow professionals can teach us a number of lessons. In this instance please consider the interactions you may have when you visit the dentist. How do the dentist's surgery procedures enable them to manage their relationship with their patients?

Look at what the dentist does when they perform work for you? How long does it take for them to be paid? More often than not the payment is made while you are on your way out through reception.

When do they arrange your next visit? Most dental receptionists are trained to book the next appointment immediately the current one has concluded.

"But that is because I know I need the next appointment," you suggest.

But accountants are no different. Your clients mostly need two 'check-ups.' The preparation of the financial statements and the annual tax return. Why not exercise the same strategy as the dentist and arrange the next meeting at the conclusion of the current one. I always book my visits to the dental surgery for the year ahead in November. Why not do this with your clients?

> **Key point:** Use the current meeting as a reason to agree the date and reason for the next meeting

HOW MANY CLIENTS DO YOU HAVE?

A clients:_____

High net worth, best clients, niche clients, those who want to see you, those who refer you.

Your definition of A clients?

....
....

B clients: _____

Those (typically) business clients that form the backbone of your client base.

Your definition of B clients?

....

....

C clients: _____

Those to whom you have no commitment or real interest in seeing you in the next twelve months. They may be your 'product clients' or those who are looked after by managers.

Your definition of C clients?

....

....

OTHERS THAT DO NOT FIT INTO THE ABOVE CATEGORIES

Some consultants have other categories such as X clients – those that you have identified to fire.

New clients in the next 12 months: _____

Okay, so you do not know how many new clients you will gain, or indeed how many you will cease to act for. However, it would be helpful to enter a realistic number and value of revenues you anticipate.

CLIENT TYPE	NUMBER	FEES GENERATED
A		
B		
C		
Others that do not fit into the above categories		
New clients in the next 12 months?		
Total		

NEW CLIENTS: A POSSIBLE MEETING PLAN FOR _____% OF MY NEW CLIENTS

Make available to all of your new clients a three-stage first year meeting plan:

First meeting

The focus of this first meeting is to get to know the client and for the firm to obtain the information it requires while identifying the services and advice the client requires.

By the time you conclude the first meeting you should establish an agenda for a second meeting. The hook? Maybe looking at their accounting systems, finding out more about their business – *"I'd really appreciate seeing you at your business premises."* Date, time and location all agreed.

Second meeting

This meeting, wherever possible, should take place at the client's premises and probably between 2-3 months after the first meeting. Clients' offices, factories etc, reveal so much about the client, their business, their values, their culture, and so on. This is not the meeting to discuss compliance matters; this is all about your client, their plans and their progress. This meeting could discuss matters such as:

- How is the business progressing compared to your expectations?
- Review the accounting records – any advice required, or affirm the client's competency in this area.
- Does the client require any advice regarding VAT or related returns?
- Are margins as expected?
- Any supplier problems, such as adequate credit terms?
- Cash flow – is there adequate working capital?
- Any trading figures available – should a flash report be prepared?
- Staffing, contractor, payroll issues?
- Feedback from customers?

And so on

Make sure they know you will write to them two months before their financial year end detailing what you need to prepare their financial statements, and that you will also meet with them around that time – the pre year end meeting.

Third meeting

The pre year-end meeting. This is the time to ensure the client knows you recognise the importance of keeping their tax liability as low as possible. As accountants, you have to work with the taxation authorities. Part of the value you offer is your firm as a highly trusted and regarded one by those bodies. Notwithstanding this, do all you can to convey to clients your commitment to ensuring their tax bill is not one penny greater than it needs to be. No one likes paying tax and one of the benefits of having to engage your services is your commitment hook, line and sinker to doing all you can to reduce their tax liability. Possible matters to discuss:

- Profit planning – what profit should the business report – opportunities for profit improvement?
- Capital expenditure – if any required should this before or after the year end?
- Remuneration planning
- Pension planning
- Tax planning
- Dividend planning
- Bonuses for employees
- What does next year's profitability look like?

This meeting also reviews the scope of records required for the completion of financial statements. Looking ahead – does the client have forecasts for the next year – working *with* the client and not just *on* the clients involves being in position as an adviser to paint the first brush strokes of the forthcoming year. Is your help required to prepare the forecasts?

A new client P.S.

Do you send out a friendly and warm email or letter before the engagement letter?

AN ANNUAL MEETING PLAN – HOW MANY MEETINGS COULD YOU HAVE WITH CLIENTS?

Client meeting calculator

Working *with* our clients not *on* them

A clients: _____

Number of times you plan to meet _____ x _____

B clients: _____

Number of times you plan to meet _____ x _____

C clients: _____

Number of times you plan to meet _____ x _____

New clients: _____

Number of times you plan to meet _____ x _____   _____

Total number of planned meetings: _____

Average meetings per month (÷12):   _____

How does this compare with meetings over the last three months:

Month_____   Meetings _____

Month_____   Meetings _____

Month_____   Meetings _____

THE CLIENT MEETING JOURNEY TAKES SHAPE

I undertook this exercise many years ago in my own firm.

After multiplying the client numbers by the planned number of meetings and adding them up, my total came to about 420 meetings.

I then divided the total client meeting count by 12 and found the answer to be 35. That meant that I could expect to have 35 client meetings a month. With each meeting lasting about an estimated hour and a quarter that accounted for 45 client hours toward my monthly target of 100 chargeable hours. But this was theory and excellent and practical as I thought it to be, what was the reality? What next? I decided to undertake some historical research...

THE STORY AS TOLD BY MY DIARY

As I turned the pages of my diary back to January, I counted the number of client meetings I had participated in. The highest number of meetings in one month had been 25. In January I had only met with clients on 15 occasions. Had I been on holiday? No. Except maybe I had failed to recognise the importance and needs of my clients. I had built a business that could manage clients' compliance needs but had I let my clients down when it came to being an adviser to whom they could turn.

YOU MANAGE WHAT YOU MONITOR

How many meetings do you plan to hold with clients in the next year? How long will you be able to spend with clients? Your existing time reporting systems should be capable of being adapted to record this time separately. You might not be able to determine what time you have spent with clients in the last year, but you should be able to track this in the next year.

You may wish to evaluate the effect of this additional chargeable time and see what the likely outcome will be. When I work with firms in this area, there are usually two common outcomes:

1. The number of potential chargeable hours from owners increases, thereby increasing utilisation. The additional meetings give rise to more chargeable time without the requirement to reduce other chargeable time.
2. The commitment to visible hours increases to such an extent that the delegation of work to managers and other team members is inevitable, potentially giving an increase in productivity and profitability.

'BUT MY CLIENTS WON'T PAY FOR THE EXTRA TIME' – THE RULE OF FEE FLEXIBILITY

Rule: Clients will pay 50 – 100 per cent more for other services than the fees they pay for compliance services so long as they can evidence the *value* and *benefit* of the additional service. Clients will pay **higher prices** if they receive **higher value**.

DO YOU STILL WONDER IF YOU CAN CHARGE FOR THIS TIME?

Yes you can. This is visible time, the client sees you face-to-face, and there is no question you are working for them. Aren't those meetings dynamic, interesting, and probing? Don't you offer solutions and bring ideas to your clients? At least with this visible time they can participate in the experience of the service, change the direction, ask questions to which they seek authoritative answers, and so on. You still have that inner self belief and confidence that it took to become an owner-accountant? Of course you can charge for your time.

QUESTIONS TO ASK YOURSELF

1

How many client meetings could you hold in the next 12 months?

2

What will your new client meeting service offer look like?

3

What additional value/revenue might this achieve?

> CLIENT **EXPERIENCE** IS THE NEXT **COMPETITIVE BATTLEFIELD** THAT IS GOING TO HELP YOU **WIN AGAINST** YOUR **COMPETITORS**.
>
> MITCH RENO, CMO, REHMANN

11 USE A CLIENT MEETING AGENDA

WHY?

The purpose of the agenda is to manage the clients' expectation regarding the scope of the meeting. As you can see from the sample agenda following, your meeting covers a range of matters that relate to your compliance work, surveys a number of current situations, and then provides an opportunity to introduce discussion on other matters.

There are alternative ways to structure an agenda, but my preference is to include a circumstantial statement followed by a question. This is often called a 'tag question'. This gives the client some perspective and insight and then poses an enquiry to gain some feedback to gauge the client's perspective on the statement.

SAMPLE MEETING AGENDA

In attendance:

....

....

Year under review – compliance matters

1. Review of accounts and clearing outstanding queries
2. Review of expenditure to confirm that all expenses that can be deducted and cost allowances have been included
3. Review of our benchmark analysis and industry trends
4. Review of our tax computations, tax saving options and the due dates for payment
5. Your feedback on our services this year. 'How well have we met your expectations?'
6. Where could we improve?

Your current year – current matters

1. How is the business currently performing?
2. What challenges do you see in the future?
3. How are the results to date compared to budget? NB: does the client have a budget, do they need up-to-date management accounts?
4. How do you see the business developing?
5. What do your competitors do that is of interest/causing you concern?
6. Are there other points of interest that you would like to discuss relating to last year's accounts?

Personal matters – two possible planning questions

1. With high property values there is now a greater liability to estate taxes. Ask, 'Would you be interested in strategies to reduce your estate taxes? Or, if the client has children and has no Will 'Do you know what will happen to the children if you both die? Who will look after them?
2. We all know about the problem of inadequate retirement funding and the importance of saving for the future. Personally, I believe that a good business owner should be financially independent of the business by the time they are 55. Have you considered what level of income you will need in retirement when the children have left, the mortgage repaid, and you have more time to pursue your other interests?' Will these interests earn you money or cost you money
3. Review services and charges – ensure the client is in tune with the value you have delivered
4. Discuss and agree our work this year and agree invoicing and payment terms
5. Discuss the services you wish us to provide in the forthcoming year
6. Agree fees and have these paid by direct debit - more to come about this later.

Other meeting questions:

1. Are there any additional services you would like to see us offer?
2. Can we help you with your business planning?
3. What else could we do to make your client experience better?

4. Are you happy with your banker and solicitor?
5. Any other matters upon that you wish to discuss?

Further client questions

Looking at last year:

1. What has your progress been like in 201x?
2. What have been your greatest challenges?
3. What has changed during the last year?
4. Has there been any change in your margins?
5. How is team morale?
6. How is your morale?
7. How have you felt about the business?
8. What was your greatest success in the last year?
9. What was your greatest failure?

QUESTIONS TO ASK YOURSELF

1

Are you persuaded about the advantage of using agendas for more of your client meetings?

2

If so, would it be advantageous to create a master template?

3

Create an agenda plan for those clients for whom you will introduce an agenda?

> IF **ANYTHING** IS **CERTAIN**, IT IS THAT **CHANGE** IS **CERTAIN**. THE **WORLD** WE ARE PLANNING FOR TODAY WILL **NOT** EXIST IN THIS **FORM** TOMORROW.
>
> PHILIP CROSBY

12 WHAT DO YOUR ACCOUNTS LOOK LIKE?

HOW MUCH USE ARE THE ACCOUNTS TO THE CLIENT?

Let me recall a story which led me to conclude that clients spend very little time looking at financial statements.

> On one occasion I visited an accounting firm and spent time with the managing partner discussing how I could be of service. I was interested to learn about their specialisations and on enquiry was told that they specialised in management accounts which they prepared for about eight clients. I was a little surprised as I regard management accounts preparation as no more than an extension of compliance work. I asked to see an example of these management accounts and was further surprised to find that these accounts comprised a single month's profit and loss account and a balance sheet in statutory format (never the easiest formats for business people to follow).
>
> *"I don't think your clients will spend more than two minutes looking at these,"* I suggested. Okay, so not the most tactful observation and indeed one that raised the hackles of my client considerably. *"What do you mean?"* He enquired. I then explained that when I produced management accounts for clients I used to produce a rolling 13 month set of accounts so that clients could not only see the results of the last month but also the corresponding month in the previous year. I moved the meeting on having realised I was, to say the least, somewhat tactless in my off the cuff observation.
>
> The following month we met again and the client started the meeting by asking me if I recalled what I had said during the previous meeting. *"Please remind me,"* I asked. *"You said you did not think my client would spend more than two minutes looking at the management accounts. After you left I called my client and made an appointment to see him. When I arrived he was sat at his desk with six unopened envelopes..."*

Some months later I visited the premises of 20 local businesses and asked them this question, *"How long do you spend looking at the accounts from your accountant?"* With only one exception the response was between one and three minutes.

During these conversations I further came to realise that business people also spend more time looking at draft accounts than they do the final accounts. By the time they receive the final accounts they have already digested as much information as they require. More about this in a moment.

If the production of financial statements is all our service is about then we are at risk from competitors who offer the same service at a lower cost and maybe quicker.

The good news is that making the step change to creating something really unique with greater value is not that difficult. All it takes is a commitment to produce the best ever looking accounts for your clients.

PRACTICE TRACK AND PRACTICEWEB

I was the founder of both these companies. Practice Track is a company specialising in publishing marketing collateral such as Budget Reports, client newsletters and tax cards while PracticeWEB is a specialist internet provider of accounting firm websites. For over 30 years my focus on every Budget Day was to do everything possible to produce a more interesting Report. Better designed. Better font. Improved features. Always innovating. I knew I could do nothing about what the Chancellor announced in his Budget Speech or the content of all the post Budget Press Notices but the teams in both companies were committed to producing a Report that we could look at, be proud of, and believe that we had just produced the 'best report ever'.

WHAT DO YOUR ACCOUNTS LOOK LIKE?

In terms of style and presentation they probably look like the accounts produced by every other firm. Why? Because we all use similar software that presents accounts as they have always been presented. Index, profit and loss account, balance sheet, notes to the accounts – all at the press of a print button. Little or no individualism. Little or no uniqueness. Little or no creativity. All about the past which is long since gone and forgotten by your clients. The following pages are ones you could produce for each of your clients in no more than sixty minutes. Please understand that I am not trying to say that this is a perfect set of accounts – you will be able to take my ideas and improve on them I am sure.

There are some underlying principles underpinning what I believe make for a significant improvement in the presentation and usefulness and value of accounts. These include:

1. The belief that clients are less interested in the past than the present and you wish to position yourself in the clients' current situation. How can you help them plan for a better tomorrow?
2. The understanding that many clients find it difficult to follow a profit and loss account or balance sheet
3. The belief that when presenting the historical report including insightful help sheets will enable you to draw your client into meaningful conversations about their future planning options.

GETTING STARTED

While some firm's deliver only electronic financial statements (into a secure document exchange environment of course) it is my firm conviction that the benefits of delivering a hard copy are immeasurable.

Imagine going shopping to both Debenhams and then Harrods. At both stores you receive you receive a bag to carry your purchases in. If you had a choice which bag would you rather be seen with? Harrods I might suggest.

Look at the perfume stalls with their products all beautifully and enticingly displayed. Manufacturers aren't into spending all that money without knowing that it will influence the purchaser. How a product is packaged makes a [big] difference.

Now, let's look revert to those draft accounts you send out. These are the ones that clients spend more time looking at. What are they printed on? Is your firm one of the many using that really high quality, no expense spared copy paper – you know the paper that routinely comes out of the main tray when the printer is flashing telling you it needs to be refilled.

First recommend: At the very least upgrade the paper you use from 80 g/m to at least 100 g/m.

Second recommend: Why not have your designer create some artwork for you to print accounts on. One version could have the word DRAFT printed in a 5-10 per cent tint across the page?

Third recommend: Why not also include a draft meeting agenda?

And now for a look at the financial statements. These are your clients' financial statements – not yours. So, permit me to share a few ideas on what you could do differently.

DOUBLE YOUR INCOME

Please note that in the following pages we have only used a spread sheet for all the figure work.

Stationery design. We have started with a business background montage onto which we are going to print the financial statements.

Cover design. Can yours be improved? Is yours looking like Primark, Debenhams or maybe Harvey Nichols or Harrods?

Binding. Can you improve how your financial statements are bound?

NOW LET'S LOOK AT SOME INDIVIDUAL PAGES

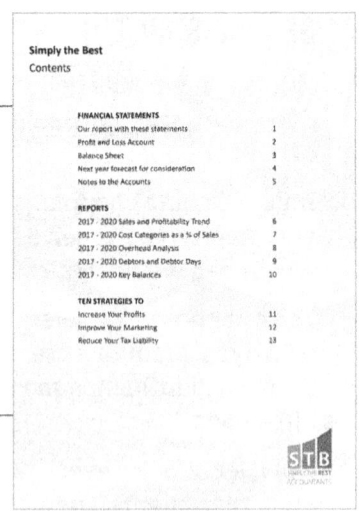

Contents

A little longer than the regular set of accounts? Looks interesting – let's explore further.

Letter to the client

These are often sent as an attachment. But your letters contain important commentary and financial information so why not include as an integral part of your reporting to your client?

WHAT DO YOUR ACCOUNTS LOOK LIKE? | 12

Profit and loss account

Nothing special here except using alternating dark and light rows to help make it easier to read the numbers across.

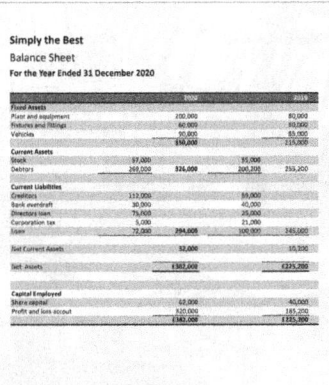

Balance sheet

The same observation applies as to the profit and loss account.

Next year forecast for consideration

This is an important page. Increase the sales and costs as you wish. The key is the final column as it enables you to discuss with the client what is currently going on in the business and to formulate a budget for the current year. Spend time with the client listening to their story of the current year – help them develop a current year budget.

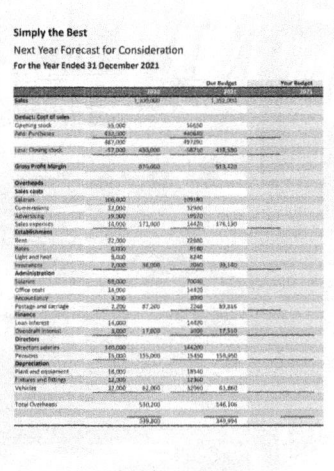

91

DOUBLE YOUR INCOME

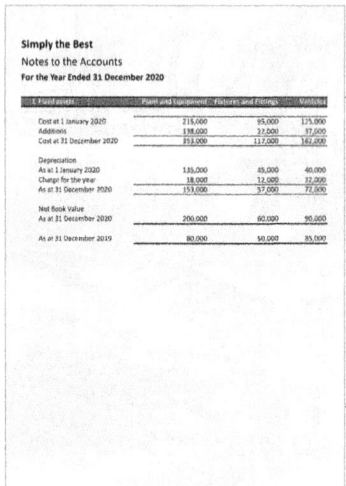

Notes to the accounts
What could you do to improve the presentation of this page?

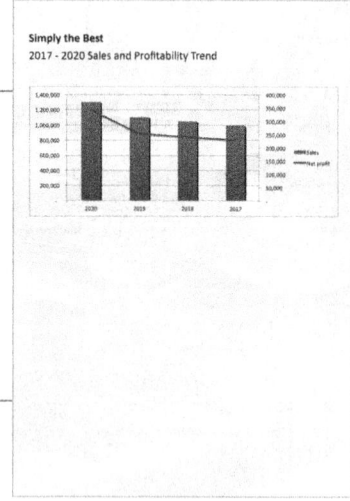

Sales and profitability trend
Extracted straight from a spreadsheet

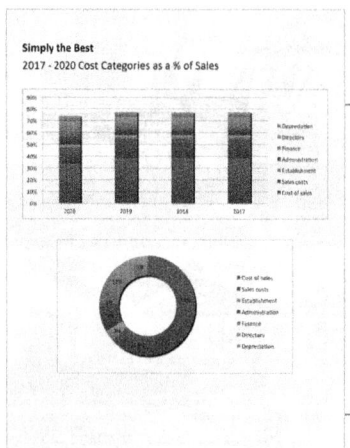

Cost categories as a percentage of sales
Extracted straight from a spreadsheet

WHAT DO YOUR ACCOUNTS LOOK LIKE? | 12

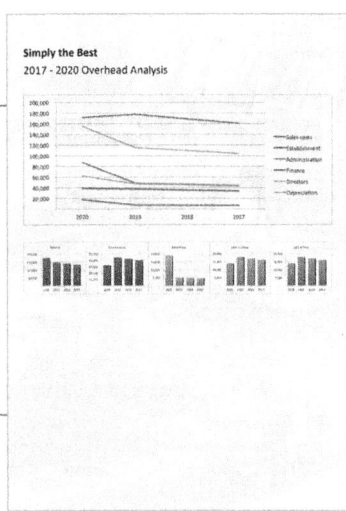

Overhead analysis
Extracted straight from a spreadsheet

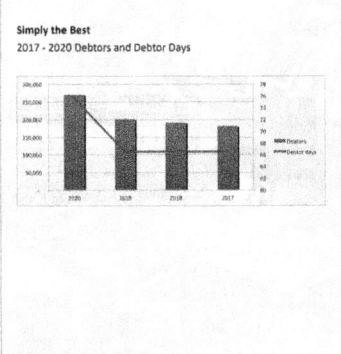

Debtors and debtor days
Extracted straight from a spreadsheet

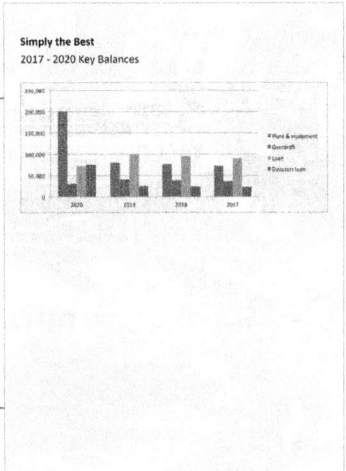

Key balances
Selection of key balances or maybe ratios

Ten strategies...to increase your profits

This report is an example of a pre written report that is intended to add value to the client. They are also there to provide a conversational springboard. Important – note the use of the QR code to link online to maybe a lengthier version of this help sheet.

A great way to remind your clients of your other services. You may wish to have one for corporates, one for unincorporated and one for tax clients

Other suggestions for your reports
- A business health check
- Ten technology pitfalls to avoid
- Ten ways to win new business
- Business ratios
- KPIs
- Key dates and deadlines
- ....
- ....
- ....

WHAT DO YOUR ACCOUNTS LOOK LIKE? | 12

QUESTIONS TO ASK YOURSELF

1

Do you need to invest in higher quality stationery for your accounts and tax returns?

2

How do you plan to improve your financial statements presentation?

3

What standard reports do you plan to create? For financial statements? For tax returns?

> WE **TRY** TO SAY **FAIL** FAST, BUT **FALL** FORWARD.
>
> JAMES POWERS, CEO, CROWE HORWATH

13 RAISING THE BAR

As a firm owner (or perhaps one destined for this job title sometime in the future) it is essential to refocus on the client experience. To recognise the clues or indicators you are transmitting to your clients. What grades are you achieving on your 'invisible report card'?

Obviously you must help solve the client's problem as no amount of good feelings can compensate for an unsolved problem. Not so obvious is that the good-feelings indicators can work synergistically with the solutions-to-problems indicators to dramatically increase the client's perception of outstanding service.

You cannot simply state your value to clients in terms of problem-solving versus price. Instead, your value **is composed of both problem-solving and emotional benefits clients receive minus the financial and non-financial burdens they bear.**

HOW DO CLIENTS JUDGE YOUR PERFORMANCE?

What clients perceive clearly defines their reality. The problem is that so much of what you do for them is not visible to them.

Clients don't see the *actual work* you do to produce the results, nor do they appreciate the technical complexity, precision, or degree of compliance expertise this work entails. The days of continuing education you invest in your team, the quality reviews your documents or reports go through, and the investment you make in your professional library every year – all of this are invisible to them.

Most clients view what accountants do as some form of magic which I call the *black tent* phenomenon. We take their records into our *sanctum sanctorum* where mere clients are never admitted, and in that inaccessible place we perform secret rites, slay secret dragons, and chant magic incantations. Eventually, we emerge from the black tent with financial reports, tax returns, and other esoteric pieces of paper that HMRC or the bank, demand of the client.

To the client, our services can appear quite unreal. They can see what they *think* is the output, the tangible representation of the service, but your input is generally incomprehensible to them.

Even though many accountants measure quality in terms of compliance with professional standards, clients know little about such standards, and care even less. The technical aspects of your service are of little interest to most clients. Occasionally they are able to perceive the service outcome – what you accomplished – but, even then, they have little clue as to how you accomplished your results in the *black tent*.

Yet clients make decisions regarding the quality of your service every time they pay your invoice. How do they do it? If they cannot judge the technical quality of your service, what criteria do they use? Just how do they decide whether you do a good job?

Let's analyse the process by which clients grade you by mentally comparing their evaluations of what they receive with what they expect.

Generally, there are eight criteria by which clients evaluate your services. The list may be longer for some clients and shorter for others. But generally clients use a combination of the following criteria:

- Timeliness
- Reliability
- Competence
- Communication
- Assurance
- Tangibles
- Responsiveness
- Empathy

Remember, clients do not necessarily evaluate these in the same way as you might do. Since much of what they need to make a full evaluation is either invisible or incomprehensible to them, they use what they can see to make a judgement about what they cannot see.

It is rather like watching sparks and lava issue from the mouth of a volcano – from what you can see you infer what you can't see – a vast reservoir of molten rock beneath the surface.

The proposition here is simple: To provide outstanding service you must exceed the client's expectations, which means what they perceive you to be doing must impress them. So, as we review and discuss these criteria below, think about how you can demonstrate your capabilities in each of these areas in ways that your clients can perceive clearly.

TIMELINESS

Of all the areas the report card highlights this is perhaps one of the most important.

> Take your car for a service and even if there is 4-5 hours work you expect to be able to collect your car at the end of the day.
>
> Order a book online – even as late as 7pm and you may expect to receive your book the next day.
>
> Order an appetiser in a restaurant and if you have to wait for more than 15 minutes you might start to become a little impatient.

These service providers and Internet suppliers all understand the importance of delivery on time, every time. The Internet has succeeding in redefining timeliness and at the same time everyone's patience levels have been reduced somewhat.

And the point?

How long do you spend actually working on clients accounting records compared to the amount of time you have them under your control? I always ask my clients to analyse their firm's performance. Without exception the perception of how long the firm takes is always less than the actuality.

Timeliness includes providing prompt service, fast turnaround, and meeting deadlines and due dates.

Questions to think about:

- What are your clients' expectations regarding your timeliness?
- How do they judge whether your delivery was timely?
- How can you improve timeliness?

RELIABILITY

Reliability is the ability to provide the promised service dependably and accurately. It includes timeliness. The client judges you on how dependable you are. It includes keeping your commitments.

Questions to think about:

- What are your clients' expectations regarding reliability? How do they judge your reliability?
- How dependable do your clients think you are? How about others in your firm?

COMPETENCE

Competence is the client's perception of your technical ability. Competence includes performing the service correctly the first time.

Questions to think about:

- What are your clients' expectations regarding competency? How do they judge your competency?
- How dependable do your clients think you are? How about others in your firm?

COMMUNICATION

Communication is how well you keep clients informed about their engagement and its outcome. It includes those aspects of client interaction where the accountant presents himself or herself as a 'great guy' or 'great lass', good adviser; knowledgeable, and so on.

Questions to think about:

- What are the client's expectations regarding communication?
- How do you know how often to talk to a client regarding an engagement in process?

ASSURANCE

Assurance is the client's feeling that their problem is in good hands. It involves the knowledge and courtesy of your frontline and their ability to convey trust and confidence. Assurance also involves credibility, which includes trustworthiness, believability, and honesty. It means having the client's best interests at heart and demonstrating care and concern. Assurance is the reason for the old saying, 'People don't care how much you know until they know how much you care.'

Questions to think about:

- How can you improve your 'bedside manner'?
- Are there aspects related to physical and financial security that need to improve?
- How good is your firm's name and its reputation?
- How good are your frontline at generating trust and confidence?

TANGIBLES

Tangibles include your physical presence, evidence and souvenirs of your service, your reception and other facilities, equipment, your website and the appearance of your personnel.

Questions to think about:
- Does your personal appearance need upgrading?
- How can you improve your tangibles for your clients? Format? Content?
- What sort of appearance do your other client-contact people present?
- Does your website need refreshing? (If not in the last month then the answer is probably 'yes'.)

RESPONSIVENESS

Responsiveness concerns your commitment to help clients and provide prompt service. Responsiveness, like reliability, also involves timeliness, accessibility, and approachability. Being responsive means:

- Clients can easily access you by telephone (lines are not busy), calls are answered promptly, and clients barely seldom put on 'hold'
- Clients do not have to navigate a computerised telephone 'receptionist' to get to you
- Appointments are easy to make and are at times clients find convenient; office hours are convenient for clients
- Waiting time in the reception area is not excessive
- Key people are not out of the office when the client needs them
- The office is conveniently located
- Clients can easily access you by direct line and/or email

Questions to think about:
- How long does it take a client to get an appointment with you?
- Are you as responsive as you could be to your clients?
- How can you improve your personal responsiveness?
- Are you as accessible to clients as you could be?
- How can you improve your accessibility?
- Do you return all telephone calls within 24 hours?

- How long does it take for you to respond to client emails?
- Does it take more than three rings before the phone is answered?
- If your clients are placed on hold, are you sure that any music or voice message are appropriate and not annoying?
- How many call screeners do your clients go through to reach you?
- Is your recorded message on your mobile a short and clear one?

EMPATHY

Empathy means you provide care and attention to clients. It goes beyond mere courtesy, although courtesy is an important part of empathy, as it is of assurance.

Questions to think about:
- What is your 'thank you quotient'?
- How do you treat the client's lower-tier employees?
- How do you think you score?

On a scale of 1 to 10 with 10 outstanding, rate yourself in each of these areas according to the score you think your clients would give you:

	HOW GOOD ARE YOU NOW?	HOW GOOD WOULD YOU LIKE TO BE?	YOUR GAP?
Timeliness			
Reliability			
Competence			
Communication			
Assurance			
Tangibles			
Responsiveness			
Empathy			

Then ask yourself, how good would you like to be? If there is improvement to be made – what can you to do to improve?

BEWARE THE PRINCIPAL CAUSES OF SERVICE FAILURES

Why do we sometimes fail to render outstanding or even merely adequate service? What causes accountants to miss the mark occasionally and get failing grades on their invisible report cards? We have identified several causes of service failures:

- Production and consumption of services partially overlap and occur simultaneously. There are inescapable interactions between frontline personnel and clients. These need to be managed from the firm's viewpoint so that the interactions are positive
- Not delivering value for money
- Inadequate service to 'internal customers' – other people in the firm
- Communication shortfalls
- Clients have unrealistic expectations of the service outcomes
- Viewing clients as 'cases' rather than people – seeing them impersonally
- Inadequate investment in technology, client interface systems and training
- Getting in 'over your head'.

How many of your service failures can be traced to one or more of these causes?

COMMUNICATION SHORTFALLS

Several types of problems occur:

1. The accountant overpromises
2. The accountant fails to stay in touch; or
3. The client misunderstands the accountant's communication.

The client may feel, 'they can't be trusted or relied on', 'I got no response', or 'my accountant doesn't listen to me. My instructions were not followed'.

FAILING TO STAY IN TOUCH WITH CLIENTS

A disproportionate number of service failures arise from accountants' failure to stay in touch with clients until a problem is resolved.

This sort of thing happens all the time – to the accountant. They are routine – to the accountant. But these are events of earthshaking importance to the client! Receipt of any notice from a taxing authority strikes fear and terror in the hearts of some clients. They may act pretty calm about it, but their guts are turning over until they get the 'all clear' from the expert. To them, these are crises comparable only to the transmission falling out of their car in the middle of a motorway at 100 miles per hour! To the accountant, it's just a routine matter.

HOW DO YOU RATE YOUR CLIENTS?

Having asked the question, *"How do your clients rate you,"* it is also good client and firm management to ask the converse question, *"How do you rate your clients?"*

The purpose of evaluating clients is not, as I perceive it, to remove clients from the firm but to identify how best to serve them profitably.

If you would like a sample of the evaluation please send me an email.

QUESTIONS TO ASK YOURSELF

How do you plan to improve timeliness? Personally? The firm?

How can you improve your communications?

What other areas do you feel need to improve?

> IT IS **BETTER** TO TAKE MANY **SMALL** STEPS IN THE **RIGHT** DIRECTION THAN TO MAKE A GREAT **LEAP** FORWARD ONLY TO **STUMBLE** BACKWARD.
>
> **CHINESE PROVERB**

14 | CLIENT CARE KPIs

On one occasion I was a participant at a conference attended by the leaders of many of the top 100 US firms. Half of the programme was speaker-led and the remainder dedicated to break out groups. I found myself unable to fully participate in the group discussions at the same level as the attendees partly because I was not in practice, not from the same country and some of these firms were grossing more than $200 million.

Toward the end of the conference we were discussing what KPIs firms were managing. The eight in my group started by sharing some of those that I recommend firms track. Debtor days, time on, billing, realisation rates, unbilled time, marketing time and so on. I listened for ten minutes and as the conversation ebbed I suggested we look at KPIs that focus on client satisfaction and levels of client service. Interestingly, my recommendation was met with a measure of incredulity, *"that's not possible to measure"* was one response. As no one else in the group supported my suggestion I decided it was wise to progress my interjection no farther. Deep within me I was surprised this was not on anyone's radar. So in this chapter allow me to explore this in a little more depth.

WHY MEASURE CLIENT SATISFACTION?

That might seem an unnecessary question but permit me to share some insights.

The purpose of any business is to meet the needs of its customers. So, doesn't it make sense to do everything possible to monitor the level of client satisfaction? If the answer to that question is 'yes' then surely there should be a means of tracking clients' views as to the level of their satisfaction? A high rating will probably mean the client happily remains with the professional service provider. Furthermore when the opportunity avails itself clients might be so enthusiastic that recommending your services to others is automatic. Do well in serving clients and this makes it more likely they will engage with your other services. Why? When your credibility and performance in the area of compliance is high then clients' are likely to view your competence in other service areas just as highly. Now, if you reflect on the principle emanating from the law of fee flexibility (Client Meetings - Chapter 10) – that is clients have a potential appetite for spending maybe up to 50-100 per cent of the compliance fee on other services, then maybe the financial driver for seeking to raise client satisfaction will motivate further consideration of the merits of enhancing and monitoring client service levels.

Conversely, a middle of the road rating may mean that almost certainly the enthusiasm to recommend or instruct you for further service is somewhat limited.

If it is known that the firm monitors client satisfaction then staff will be more aware and endeavour to do what they can to improve their performance.

WHY FIRMS DON'T HAVE ANY KPIS

So, if serving clients is what we do and we don't monitor performance levels we might ask *"why not?"*

There are a number of common reasons often revolving around:

1. The perception or belief that a client survey is a one-off event that demands too great an investment of resources
2. Thinking that it won't tell us anything we do not already know, and
3. The sense that we are not in a good place right now and we don't want to hear [more] bad news.

Because most firms currently have an automatic right to work on a client's behalf every year this entitlement can cause accountants to be sluggish or lethargic when it comes to going the extra mile. In addition, some accountants have so much work they are not motivated to become too involved with work that is not compliance.

CLIENT SURVEY

Firms who have sent out client surveys report that often they only receive 15 to 20 per cent back. So what do the other 80 to 85 per cent think? Now, you are unlikely to receive a 100 per cent response but you should do all you can to approach this in such a way as to raise the response levels.

Many of the client surveys I have seen are too lengthy – some even longer than a tax return or the tax enquiry questionnaire that firms send out to clients. Furthermore, many firms that undertake an *annual* survey have averaged three, maybe four, over a ten year period! So, let's see how we can fix that. Before we go into more detail, let us look at some of the responses from some of the surveys I have conducted for accounting firms:

- We do not get on with the [engagement] partner
- We are going to look for another accounting firm
- We have business problems but no one has come back to us after we called asking for help
- Names and contact details of people to contact who might be interested in a new accountant
- Dissatisfaction with bank
- Dissatisfaction with lawyer
- Dissatisfaction with financial adviser
- We are just about to lodge a claim against you!

As well as:

- The partner we work with is really very helpful
- We have recommended you on a number of occasions
- We are interested in your other services
- Would you be able to present the recent seminar I attended to my other directors?
- Great work, great people.

It is possible to fill many pages with the feedback from surveys, but the point is, do you see the value in all the above comments? I trust you do!

It has been said that 'feedback is the breakfast of champions,' and as good business people it is your responsibility to allow clients to express their view on your services – they deserve to be heard and you should give them the opportunity to express their satisfaction or dissatisfaction. The question is 'how can you institutionalise client feedback'?

INSTITUTIONALISING CLIENT FEEDBACK

Learn the lesson from other service providers. We are all asked to evaluate service providers such as hotels, tour operators and the garage's service department. They all want to know how they performed and whether or not the customer was satisfied. We are, of course, never asked to rate any of the utility companies, the local authority, the supermarkets or local shops – although maybe they could benefit from feedback, or maybe they think they have such an automatic right to business that they don't care – or in the case of the local shops they are just not geared up to do something that would probably annoy customers.

You can approach securing client feedback in a number of ways:

1   In reception

Your receptionist meets all your clients and he or she probably sees them sitting in reception for five or more minutes whenever they visit your office. Just before the client sits down, this question could be asked *"would you mind spending a minute or two to answer a few questions about our services?"* Most people will respond affirmatively so they can then be handed a brief questionnaire – see below for some suggested questions. The completed response can then either be posted into a 'Feedback Please' box in reception or returned to the receptionist in a sealed envelope.

2   After a job has been completed

This approach requires you to give or send a questionnaire after the completion of your work – this could be after the completion of the financial statements or the tax return. If you are expecting the response to be posted then provide a postage paid envelope.

3   Your website

Some firms now send clients a link to an area on their website where online feedback can be provided.

4   Apps

In the future you will be able to use an app to harness client feedback.

TAKING ACTION

There is a golden rule that every client should be thanked for completing a survey form. Maybe you could either call, or send a free report the client might be interested in – or both. If the client has expressed any dissatisfaction then address that immediately, thanking them for their willingness to share their concern. The key is to acknowledge their responses – that is one of the hallmarks of a firm that puts clients' interests first. It takes effort, but that is minimal if the firm has a culture of really caring about clients and the quality of service delivered.

Suggested word form for your surveys? It is my belief that the form of wording below provides clients with the opportunity to express any feedback they care to offer.

CLIENT SURVEY

We know that successful business relationships require an open and honest dialogue, please help us improve our services by completing this brief six-question survey

1. Are there any areas where you are dissatisfied with our service?

2. So that we can improve, can you tell us what we need to do differently?

3. We aim to bring real value to you as a client and to help you achieve success on your terms. To what extent have we helped/advised you in the past year?

4. Our goal is to help you achieve your personal and business objectives. Where do you want to be in a year's time?

5. What would it mean to you to achieve these goals?

6. What more can we do to help you in the next year?

Thank you.

> Your feedback helps us ensure that our services are in line with your expectations and needs. If you would like to meet to discuss your responses to any of the above, please let us know.
>
> Is there anyone you believe would benefit from our services and expertise? If so, please use the space below to provide contact information or do please call me/us directly on _____ (firm number)

TAX SAVED FOR CLIENTS

So far as clients are concerned, one of the essential expectations they have is that they will pay the absolute lowest amount of tax possible – no one wishes to pay a penny more tax than necessary.

But, do you know how much tax you have saved clients over the last year? I know some firms that track the cumulative tax they save clients on a firm-wide basis each year. They aim to save, say, £1 million a year – something they are keen to promote with their clients, prospects and firm advocates. Some accountants have written articles promoting the emphasis they place on quantifying tax saved for clients.

TIME TO COMPLETE THE JOB

We have already looked at this in the previous chapter but it is worth revisiting in the context of monitoring the elapsed time the records are with you as a KPI.

Go to the dentist and you are likely to be out in less than 30 minutes. Take your car in for a service and you will [probably] have it back by the end of the day. Take your books and records to the accountant and you will have the job completed... when it is finished!

While some firms plan to turn jobs around in a month others have no commitment other than to do the job as soon as possible. The fact that average firm lock up is somewhere in the 100 day region confirms that many firms are not performing timely work and neither are they being paid in a timely way. This 20th century model is broken and as a consequence needs fixing. How? It all starts with mission, vision, planning, commitment and execution.

LET'S LOOK AT ONE FIRM'S RECORDS

Let's look at five typical jobs from one of my client's offices and identify how long it took to complete the work compared to the total time the records were available to work on. To do this the client records when the job first becomes available to start and when the work is completed. Then we look at the number of hours to complete that job and convert that into days.

Case study

TIME TO COMPLETE WORK IN THE OFFICE

	Client	Date job available to start	Date job completed	Days in our control	Hours to complete	Days to complete	% time on job
1	ABC	1 February	28 March	56	84	12	21
2	DEF	15 February	18 March	31	91	13	42
3	GHI	28 February	23 March	23	49	7	21
4	JKL	2 March	14 April	43	140	20	38
5	MNO	6 April	2 June	57	189	27	47
				210		79	37

TIMELINESS OF SERVICE IS KEY

As you can see these five jobs were in the firm's control for 210 days and were left unworked on for 131 (210-79) days. Overall these five jobs were worked on for 37 per cent of that time. What should this be? I am reluctant to give an answer to this question, but I think a benchmark should be established and everyone aware that timeliness is a really important issue.

We are not prepared to wait in a doctor or dentist's waiting room for more than 15 minutes before we become a little concerned, even annoyed. We certainly don't like being without our car for a routine service for more than a day – maybe two. A timely service means the books can be returned earlier and the service paid for quicker. If you don't redefine your focus and set targets then nothing is going to change.

SOME SUGGESTIONS TO HELP YOU ACHIEVE A TIMELIER TURNAROUND

Contact clients six or eight weeks before their financial year end and give them a checklist of what you require to complete the preparation of their tax or financial statements. You will probably start with a standard checklist but this will need personalising. Maybe the last task on a job is to update the list of client-required information for the subsequent year.

You should:

1. Indicate a date when you expect to receive these records – an 'appointment' for the records to come into your 'waiting room'
2. Call or maybe text a reminder two weeks before confirming the date the client has agreed to provide the records
3. On receipt of the records have someone check that the records are complete.

Write to the client and send the list of records you have received with a provisional date for the review of the draft accounts (that is a scary move for some firms). How would you feel if you ordered a meal in a restaurant and it was 30 minutes before the starter arrived? And then another 45 minutes before the main course arrived? That happened to me once in a 5 star hotel and after lodging a complaint and receiving no feedback I asked to meet with the manager. Thankfully (for him) he was fully briefed on the complaint and he volunteered that the standard of service was unacceptable. Without me asking, he offered a complimentary meal to my wife and I that evening in the hotel's best restaurant. Poor timeliness cost the hotel. Is there a cost for poor timelines for the accountant? I think so. Poor timeliness results in a higher level of lock up (debtors and WIP). Poor timeliness gives the client less time to be aware of what has to be saved for future tax liabilities.

On the other hand, when everyone is aware of the importance of timeliness, effort will focus on performance and all the above negatives will be reversed. Timeliness provides the opportunity to do some more up-to-date tax planning or management accounts.

1. Have staff schedule review finalisation work with the manager and partner
2. Prepare firm-wide reports that evidence the firm's performance each month
3. Partners: when you do your MBWA (managing by wandering about) ask staff if they are experiencing any job problems
4. I was working with one client whose staff were surveyed prior to a retreat. One of the key issues raised was the problem experienced with clients not responding promptly with answers to queries or supplying additionally requested information. Also, staff were uncertain whether to make contact by email or telephone. As a result, a standard policy was introduced which has been very effectively implemented. The time taken to complete jobs has reduced by more than 20 per cent. And they are still improving.

ONE FIRM INTRODUCED THIS POLICY

> ### Timeliness of service
>
> We seek to do all we can to complete the work undertaken for clients as soon as possible. After the client has provided the necessary records it is possible that responding to our requests for help may not be top of the clients' 'must do' list. This is especially the case if the work does not start within a few days of the records being received in the office. Without us harassing our client the following procedures should be observed by staff working on the job:
>
> Check that the job has been booked in and that an initial review has been completed confirming that all records have been received.
>
> When you start the job please call our client and advise them you will be working on the preparation of their financial statements.
>
> When you identify a requirement for further information make sure you have done all you can to collate as many points as possible, then call the client. Introduce yourself and ask *"is this a convenient time to talk?"* When you have the client's permission detail what you require and confirm, if necessary, that you will put this in writing. Most importantly, ask the client for confirmation of when the information will be available. Your request should be framed politely, for example: *"Would it be possible to have this information by..."* If the client feels unable to agree our timeline, ask the client to state when they expect to be able to provide the information. Always end calls with a 'thank you'.
>
> It is our recommendation not to call clients more than twice without being put through to the relevant person. After two calls we recommend you email the client and advise *"I have called in order to ask for further information to enable me to progress the completion of your financial statements/tax return, would it be possible for you to give me a call on .... in order to briefly discuss the further information we require?"*

Does this work every time? No. But this policy has seen a significant reduction in elapsed time to complete the job and an improvement in staff morale as the frustration of having four or more jobs in progress at any one time has been greatly reduced.

You will have to accept that this will not always work as there will always be clients that do not cooperate. Having said that, maybe they are the clients that should perhaps look for another service provider.

THREE OTHER KPIs?

1. Some firms monitor the number of client meetings
2. Others the value of additional work performed for clients
3. Others monitor the value of new client referrals.

The key to deciding which ones are appropriate for you is to focus on those areas where you wish to commit to improving client service. If you come up with some good ones, do please email them to me at: mark@marklloydbottom.com.

QUESTIONS TO ASK YOURSELF

1
How do you plan to monitor client satisfaction?

2
What other KPIs do you find important?

3
You manage what you monitor – what else do you plan to monitor?

> YOU CAN **NEVER PLAN** THE **FUTURE** BY THE **PAST**.
>
> EDMUND BURKE

15 TOP LINE MANAGEMENT

THERE ARE FIVE FACTORS THAT AFFECT YOUR PRICES

Only five things affect the amount you can charge for your services:

1. Demand for what you do
2. How easily someone can replace you
3. Your ability – or efficiency
4. Return on investment (ROI) of resources – or effectiveness

Effectiveness is 'doing the right things right'. An individual's resource is his or her time. A firm's resource is employee and owner time. Owners improve their ROI with better time management, delegation, supervision of team members, and better client selection and client management.

5. The fifth factor…

The willingness to demand it. Have the courage to demand what you are worth.

THE KEY IS TOP LINE MANAGEMENT

1. Enhancing revenue instead of reducing costs
2. Not compromising on prices

> **Key point:** A well managed and profitable firm will normally have a realisation rate of 85% of standard charge rates.

HOW TO MAKE 'BALANCED' CHANGES

You can increase effective charge out rates by either:

1. Maintaining the same realisation rate and increasing your average standard charge out rate, or
2. By maintaining the same standard charge out rates and increasing realisation.

Often, the best way to produce the desired increase in effective charge out rates with the least change in operations is to make balanced changes in each of these two areas.

Current realisation less than 85% - increase prices

If your current realisation is less than 85%, I would agree that an increase in charge out rates may not be appropriate, provided you target an immediate increase in realisation of at least 5%.

Current realisation above 85% - increase charge rates

If your current realisation is at or above 85%, your entire increase in effective charge out rates should be from higher charge out rates. Let your realisation remain where it is or even drift down a little to the low 80s. My empirical observation is that the highest effective charge out rates seem to be achieved with higher standard charge out rates and realisation in the mid 80s.

If you do it the right way, you can normally increase charge out rates 10 to 15% for employees and 10 to 20% for some owners without clients even noticing the change.

"But we can't possibly do that the increase is too great." This is feedback I often hear so please allow me to address this point head-on as the feedback is understandable but fundamentally flawed.

First, you are only increasing the charge rates and not the prices you charge clients.

Second, if this view of impossibility persists then divide the increase by either 6, 9 or 12 and increase charge rates by small increments each month. That way the increases will be infinitesimal.

So, reverting back to point 1 – what is the point of doing this if prices do not increase?

Again, an important point that needs addressing. Your time recording system is nothing other than a retail costing system but, to the extent that you are still charging based on time, it is a powerful tool that indicates what is fair – fair to the firm and fair to the client.

It remains a fact there are no list prices for our compliance services (although this will change over time), so your time records often determine your perception of what is fair. If the time on is higher some of that time may be billed. If it is not there in front of you then it never will.

A car engine, when finely tuned and balance will tick over at between 600 and 1,000 rpm.

A finely balanced costing system is finely tuned and delivering maximum power when the firm's realisation rate is within striking distance of 85%.

QUESTIONS TO ASK YOURSELF

1
What is your firm's realisation rate?

2
Do you need to increase prices?

3
Do you need to increase charge rates or client quotes?

> **PLANNING** IS A PROCESS OF **CHOOSING** AMONG THOSE MANY **OPTIONS**. IF WE DO **NOT** CHOOSE TO **PLAN**, THEN WE **CHOOSE** TO HAVE **OTHERS** PLAN **FOR** US.
>
> RICHARD I. WINWOOD

16 AGREEING PRICES WITH CLIENTS

Many accountants somehow have the idea that it is unprofessional to discuss prices with clients. Perhaps they think it gives clients the wrong impression that the accountant is primarily concerned with money. Yet no one wants to buy something with no idea of the price.

When you go into a store, who brings up the subject of price? The store. They do it by attaching price tags to everything. When you go to a garage, who first mentions the price? The petrol station. They post their prices on signs and on the pumps. These are the signs that have told us all just how much fuel has increased in recent years. When you are interested in buying a building, who starts the price negotiation? The seller does, by listing an asking price.

> **Key point:** If goods and services are being sold, the seller has the responsibility to mention the price first.

Even if the price will be subject to negotiation – such as property or used cars – the seller opens the negotiation with an asking price.

For people whose very language of business is money, accountants demonstrate an amazing reluctance to discuss prices.

> **Key point:** Many clients are embarrassed to mention price because they believe it will make them appear unsophisticated. They are relieved when you bring up the subject.
>
> If the accountant is also too embarrassed to discuss prices, a disaster could be waiting for both accountant and client. As mentioned earlier...

> **Key point:** Clients accept value pricing better than most accountants do – if – and only if – you discuss the price with them before you perform the service.

Whether you discuss prices or not, the client has some price in mind. It's hard enough to meet a client's expectation if you know them; it's impossible if you don't even know what price range they are considering. Therefore, it's just good business to discuss price with clients before committing any firm resources to the project.

> **Key point:** Avoid the word fee when speaking to clients, prospects, and referral sources. Instead, say price. People sometimes perceive fees to be more negotiable than prices.

TRAIN YOUR CLIENTS TO PAY YOU WELL AND PROMPTLY

What "How much is this going to cost?" really means

When clients enquire regarding the cost of the service they are most likely seeking to establish what they should budget, or if this is a service they can afford. It is easy to hear a subliminal message that this is, perhaps, a service they cannot afford or that you are too expensive. For some it takes courage to ask a professional what it will cost, but given that, mostly accountancy services can't currently be easily compared, we should answer the question by giving the client an estimate range and indicate the proviso(s) with regard to the lower end estimate.

Your pricing communicates your value

If you price your services at the low end of the market, clients won't take you seriously. If you are expensive, not only will they respect you, they are more likely to implement your recommendations because they paid so much for them.

> **Example:** When I first went into practice, Bob Bennett, a very successful managing partner in Bristol, taught me to answer the question, *"How much do you charge?"* by saying *"We are as expensive as anyone, and our clients think we are worth it."*

> **Key point:** The more people pay for something, the more valuable it is.

Naturally, you should always discuss price before you perform a service. This is not only common courtesy; it is also good business. You have greater leverage with a client before you perform a service because the client wants something from you (a solution to a problem). After you perform the service, the client has greater leverage because you want something from the client (money).

One important factor affecting the client's perception of your value is your own attitude toward your prices. Just as some animals can 'smell fear', clients can often sense if you are uncomfortable with your own prices. They observe – often unconsciously – your tone of voice, the words you choose, the loudness of your voice, your body language, even your breathing. If you are ambivalent or wishy-washy, a good negotiator will sense that and press the advantage to lower your prices.

On the other hand, if you are comfortable with your value and your prices, clients will also sense that and they, too, will feel confidence in your value. I learned this simple truth from one of my own clients.

Key point: What you say with confidence, they will believe!

Most clients will pay a fair price. They are chiefly concerned that other clients pay comparable prices. Clients periodically need reassurance that the firm charges all its clients fairly – maybe not cheaply, but fairly.

HOW TO USE LLOYDBOTTOM'S LAW AND LLOYDBOTTOM'S COROLLARY

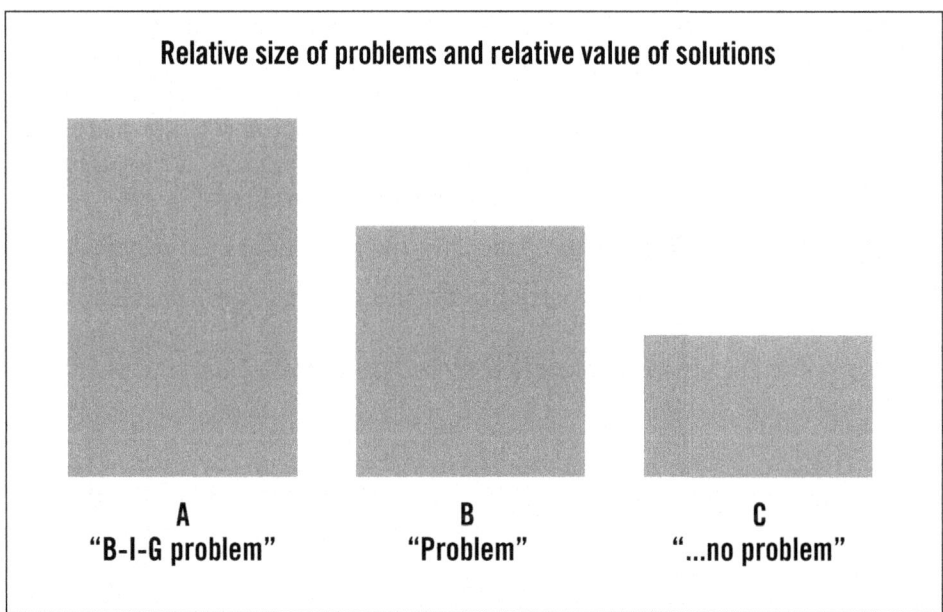

When a client receives a letter from the taxman which highlights questions the tax authorities require the answer to – the letter is never dismissed lightly.

If it is one page long, the eyebrows may not be overly raised - especially if it is clear that only a minor point requires clarification. However, if the letter is two or three pages long it is likely that some degree of concern – maybe even alarm takes hold.

A visit to the accountant is quickly arranged.

Let's look at two approaches at either end of the spectrum:

Approach 1

The accountant: *"John, (the client) I have also received a copy of the letter from the tax office and was going to contact you. I know it is a long letter but don't worry we will take care of it for you. No need for you to worry. I will be in contact with you as we are likely to need to do some research and might need to discuss some of the points raised in the letter. Please be assured that we will deal with all of this for you, so don't worry."*

Approach 2

"John, I am contacting you having seen the letter from the tax office as I thought this was a matter that we urgently need to discuss. The tax office has been sending a number of letters like this recently and it is clear they have a campaign on at present. This type of enquiry sometimes takes up to a couple of years to settle – the tax office seems to keep coming up with requests for additional information time after time. Please be assured I will deal with this on as timely a basis as possible. If there is any further tax liability the tax office will seek to add a penalty and interest to any outstanding tax – so it is in everyone's interest to attend to this as soon as possible. At this stage it is not possible to forecast the likely additional tax, if any, that may be payable but be assured I will do everything I can to ensure this is kept to a minimum."

Contrast the difference between these differing approaches to the same letter.

The lesson according to Lloydbottom's law and Lloydbottom's corollary?

> **Key point:** A client's problem is always bigger to the client than it is to you.

> **Key point:** Lloydbottom's law: The value of the solution varies with the size of problem.

> **Key point:** Lloydbottom's corollary: The bigger the problem, the more valuable the solution.

> **Key point:** If you minimise the size of the problem, you minimise the value of your solution.

THE PROBLEM WITH PRICE ESTIMATES

Price estimates are just that, but accountants often fail to communicate that to clients. Clients are given the impression that an estimate is a fixed price even though that was not what was intended. Even a regular client, who understands that your quote is only an estimate, will eventually lose confidence if the final prices consistently exceeds the estimates.

Accountants are usually better off estimating a project on the high side and then giving the client a pleasant surprise. Then they will learn that the estimate is usually a worst case.

The danger, especially with new clients, is that a high estimate will, in fact, prompt them to look elsewhere. So, they never become regular clients.

To prevent this, accountants should give the estimate as a range, carefully explain all the variables, and explain to the client what he or she can do to help keep the price low.

HOW TO AVOID PROFESSIONAL PANIC

Some accountants get panicked by what is going on in the lowest 10 per cent of the market.

> **Key point:** Focus on the 90-plus per cent of your clients who are very happy with your prices and your service. You never hear from them about how reasonable they think your prices are, so you often forget they are there.

ASK FOR AN ADVANCE PAYMENT – A DEPOSIT

Always ask for a payment in advance from a new client as evidence of his or her commitment to the relationship. If clients are unwilling to pay a portion of your price before the service, he or she may be unwilling to pay after the service. An up front payment requirement also serves as part of the screening process for new clients.

BE FLEXIBLE

Be flexible in your terms and make it easy to buy. For instance, it's okay to take credit cards. Most clients who engage you don't have cash-flow problems, but occasionally one will have a problem with a request for a deposit to confirm your engagement. If your conflict of interest checks and due diligence disclose no other problems with the client, you may accommodate him or her. As long as your clients pay the agreed price for your yearly services over the year you deliver them, I don't see a problem. For instance, if you are negotiating with a retailer who is cash-strapped in a particular season, they may prefer to match their payments to their cash flow. Some people prefer to pay monthly or quarterly, depending on when their customers pay them.

IMPORTANT TOOLS IN NEGOTIATING PRICES

Who initiated the need? If the client called you, you can charge more.

1. The eyebrow test - watch their body language for signs that you have reached their upper fee level expectations
2. Ask "How much have you budgeted to solve this problem?" Ask the client what the price should be, or how much it is worth. Value is in the eyes of the client. If he or she sees £1,000 of value for a job that will cost £15,000 to do, better find out before you do the job.
3. If I can save you £5,000, how much of the savings/extra money/etc. are you willing to share with me?

How to handle price objections

Never sell on price or cut your fee. Once you do that, they will never be good clients.

Instead, just ask:

"Do you know what it will cost you if you don't do it?"

For estate planning, you may joke that it won't cost them anything; it will cost their kids.

If the client continues to object, say this:

"Our fee is a minor investment compared to what you can save (or make or gain)."

This again places their attention on results instead of the cost.

Then, go into what they will gain, depending on the nature of the engagement. Whether the service will be succession planning, retirement planning, a new accounting system, or whatever, you should paint a vivid picture for the client of how rosy the future can be if they solve this problem.

Alternatively, you might also paint a picture of how bad it could be if they do not solve the problem.

Keep them thinking about what they will gain or save, not about your price.

"If you neglect tax planning, it's like saying you would rather HMRC get your money than yourself or your own children and grandchildren."

HOW TO HANDLE PROCRASTINATORS

Some clients don't like to make decisions. They will say *"I have to study the issue and sleep on it before I make a decision,"* or *"I'm going on holidays. I'll do it later,"* or *"I am very busy for the next eight weeks. Let's talk about it when I'm freed up."*

Here is a selection of concerns you could express:

"If anything happens to you between now and then, I would hate myself for letting you delay. Changes in your circumstances could foreclose some options you now have; they might no longer be available. The longer you wait, the more risk you take that you will be left with fewer choices. You may lose a key employee, your building could catch fire, you could become uninsurable, you might get disabled. Who knows what the future holds? You will sleep better at night once you handle this. Do it now."

HOW TO HANDLE PRICE COMPLAINTS

How many of your clients are really complaining?

- Make sure it is a complaint and not a comment.
- *"Who knows? Maybe he will lower the price. It cannot hurt to ask."*

For *real* complaints, ask

- *"Why do you think it is too high?"*

Nine out of ten times, when a client does complain about a price, the price is not the real problem, say

- *"Evaluate us over one to two years."*
- *"We are worth three times what we cost."*

Allow for value pricing in your engagement letters

You can and should invoice many routine engagements based on value to the client rather than time charges. Even in routine engagements, allow for value pricing in the engagement letter terms.

Unfortunately many firms' standard engagement letter terms do not allow for invoicing above standard charge out rates, even where justified. Instead they will include a price provision such as: *"Our prices are based on the time we devote to an engagement."*

Here is appropriate illustrative language:

> **Example:** We generally base our prices on the time required at our regular charge out rates for the services and personnel assigned plus out-of-pocket costs [Note the use of the word generally which allows for exceptions.]

> **Example:** However, our charges also might include other appropriate factors, including the difficulty of the assignment, how much risk and responsibility the work entails, time limitations imposed on us by others, the experience and professional expertise of the personnel assigned, and the priority and importance of the work to the client.

> **Example:** Assuming adequate records, internal controls, and assistance of your personnel, we estimate that our price for the [services] will range between £_____ and £_____. We will attempt to minimise our charges without sacrificing the quality of our work. The extent to which this can be done will depend on the availability of your personnel to offer us clerical and other assistance in preparing schedules, performing analyses, and providing source documents. If we encounter any significant unusual circumstances not contemplated in preparing the estimate, we will discuss it with you and arrive at a new price estimate before we incur additional costs. [Accountants often omit these contingencies from engagement letters, making it easy for the client's personnel to avoid helping the accountant.]

> **Example:** These estimated prices are based on the assumption that you will continue to employ competent, experienced bookkeeping personnel. If a change in your personnel requires us to spend extra time to train your people or otherwise perform our services, we will invoice you for such extra time. [You might use this language for a client who has had high staff turnover in the accounting department.]

When value pricing opportunities arise, discuss the price with the client before you begin work and obtain his or her agreement about how you will invoice the engagement. One of our clients obtained a £10,000 write up on one engagement by following this recommendation.

QUESTIONS TO ASK YOURSELF

1

What proportion of your fees are already agreed taking into account the likelihood that the next year's prices will be based on the fee for the previous year?

2

If others in the firm are quoting different rates would an internally agreed set of minimum fees be helpful?

3

Which clients do you need to meet to agree a price adjustment?

> **REDUCE** YOUR **PLAN** TO **WRITING**.
> THE **MOMENT** YOU **COMPLETE** THIS, YOU WILL HAVE DEFINITELY GIVEN **CONCRETE** FORM TO THE **INTANGIBLE** DESIRE.
>
> **NAPOLEON HILL**

17 THE EMERGING ROLE OF THE PRICING DIRECTOR

At the 2014 Prime Symposium (held in USA with invited attendees) one of the hottest sessions was the one devoted to the emerging role of the Pricing Director in professional firms. Attendees to this conference are mainly the Managing Partners of the top 200 USA accounting firms and attendance is by invitation only.

Following the presentation by Stuart Dodds, the Pricing Director of a top ten USA law firm the discussion tables were buzzing. Of the 90 attendees it is reckoned that maybe as many as half of them planned to return to the next Conference having appointed a Pricing Director.

ARTICLE WRITTEN ABOUT SMARTER PRICING, SMARTER PROFITS
by Jonathan Groner, Capital Ideas Newsletter

Now that concepts such as price negotiation, legal project management, and procurement have forever become part of daily life at major law firms, it's time for a book that presents the ideas behind them clearly and non-technically to professionals who need to understand them on a day-to-day basis. This effort by Stuart Dodds, director of global pricing and legal project management at Baker & McKenzie, is that book.

Dodds starts, where he should, with the rise of the 'new normal.' Now that law firms are constantly competing for work on the basis of price among other factors, a knowledge of pricing – how to set a price, how to actually receive that desired price, and how to manage a matter once a price has been set – is indispensable.

Dodds' chapters on legal project management (LPM) demonstrate a practical, in-depth knowledge of the subject. They also provide an explicit link between LPM, budgeting, and the new normal: *"There is an increasing expectation,"* he writes, *"that law firms also begin to stick to the agreed budget, with this budget now effectively becoming a cap. (Given how some law firms actually manage their matters, this for some has come as a shock.)"*

His approach to starting an LPM program is straightforward: *"Keep it simple – initially focus your efforts around the people, then processes, and only then the systems.... Take the mystery out of LPM and put back the pragmatism. Don't over analyse it – it is better to do something, try it, refine it, and then do something else."*

Dodds writes clearly and pretty much stays away from financial jargon and consultant-speak. When he presents a chart, he explains it non-technically and without equations. He seems to be keeping in mind that most of his readers will not have a background in finance or accounting. In fact, I think the readers who will most benefit from the book are law firm managers and practice group leaders.

Before entering the law firm world, Dodds worked in consulting, including 14 years at Accenture. Because of that background, he's not afraid to discuss the 'p' word when it comes to law firms – and here I mean not so much price as procurement. While many lawyers still see procurement as irrelevant or even dangerous to the business of law, Dodds embraces it and empathises with procurement professionals since he once was one himself:

"Those in procurement are looking for the tangible outcomes from the successful tender, they are looking for proof and the ability to measure (in part so they can quantify their own contribution), they are seeking evidence that you can do what you say you can do, they want to be able to quickly quantify the overall organizational return on investment, and finally, they want 'demonstrable value,'" he writes.

On the other hand, Dodds recognises that that the procurement mentality isn't infallible. He tells the story of a senior lawyer who was asked to visit the procurement office of a client to finalise a contract.

The procurement head demanded that the firm immediately agree to reduce its hourly fee by at least 15 per cent. The lawyer reminded the procurement head that his law firm was being hired to protect the company from a potential multi-million dollar claim and started to walk out. Dodds' conclusion is that in this instance, the client's *"inexperienced procurement people"* had *"mistaken price for value."*

The book is full of anecdotes like this that help ensure that the book's messages about how to set a price, get a price, and adhere to the price are not forgotten.

Smarter Pricing, Smarter Profit
published by the American Bar Association
www.smarterpricing.org.

CHAPTER OUTLINES

Chapter 1:
Introducing Our Framework:

Chapter 2:
The Rise of the New Normal

Chapter 3:
Law Firm Economics 101: How Law Firms Make Money

'Growth Is Dead' Watching the Revenue Line Productivity Matters (But Perhaps Not as Much as You Think!). The Magic Ingredient to Better Profitability and Happier Clients: Leverage Profitability: A Meaningful Measure? Step One: Set the Price

Chapter 4:
Pricing and the Question of Value: The Limitations of Traditional Pricing Models. The Concept of 'Price' The Steps to Implementing Value Pricing. Types of Price The 'Right' Price. The Impact of Price. The 1-3-4 Rule. The Management of Pricing

Chapter 5:
Getting Started: Beginning with the End in Mind. Scoping the Opportunity. Determining the Options. Competition and Resisting the 'Race to the Bottom.' Gaining Approval.

Chapter 6:
Demystifying AFAs: What They Really Are and How They Really Work Speaking the Same Language: A Question of Terminology. Finding an Appropriate Model. Looking at Our Options in More Detail. Risk-Mitigating Approaches. Firm Considerations. Client Considerations. Discounted Hourly Rates. The Basic Outline. Law Firm and Client Considerations. Blended or Banded Hourly Rates. The Basic Outline. Law Firm Considerations. Client Considerations.

Cost-Driven Approaches

Fixed or Flat Fees. The Basic Outline. Law Firm Considerations Client Considerations Variations on a Theme In Summary

Retainer-Based Fees. The Basic Outline. Law Firm Considerations Client Considerations

Capped Fees. The Basic Outline. Law Firm Considerations Client Considerations Variations on a Theme In Summary

Value-Aligned Approaches Performance-Based Fees. The Basic Outline. Law Firm Considerations Client Considerations

Contingent or Conditional Fees The Basic Outline. Law Firm Considerations. Client Considerations Variations on a Theme

In Summary Value-Driven Pricing. The Basic Outline. Law Firm Considerations Client Considerations Variations on a Theme

In Summary... And Not Forgetting. Volume Discounts. The Basic Outline. Law Firm Considerations. Client Considerations. So what does it all mean?

Chapter 7:
The Power of Pragmatic Analysis

Chapter 8:
There and Back Again: A Question of Value

Chapter 9:
The Two Ps: Part 1

Chapter 10:
The Two Ps: Part 2

Chapter 11:
Preparing for Your Negotiation

Chapter 12:
Conducting Your Negotiation

Chapter 13:
The Rise of Legal Project Management

Chapter 14:
Thinking Big, Starting Small

Chapter 15:

Getting It Right from the Start

Chapter 16:

Bringing It All Together

Chapter 17:

Maintaining the Momentum: During the Matter

Chapter 18:

Making the Right Lasting Impression

Chapter 19:

All Feedback Is Good Feedback: Getting Even Better

Chapter 20:

Metrics that Matter

Chapter 21:

The Chicken and the Egg

Chapter 22:

The Role of Technology and the Rise of Big Data

Chapter 23:

The Corporate Mentality: The Changing Nature of Practice

Reprinted with permission from Smarter Pricing, Smarter Profit available for purchase from: shopaba.org 2014(c) by the American Bar Association. All rights reserved. This information or any or portion thereof may not be copied or disseminated in any form or by any means or stored in an electronic database or retrieval system without the express written consent of the American Bar Association or the copyright holder.

SAMPLE JOB DESCRIPTION

Director of Strategic Pricing Job in Kansas City, MO

ABC's decision to relocate its Global Services Center to Kansas City means an influx of new job opportunities for the city. Because ABC needs to hire such a large and diverse group of new professionals, they formed an exclusive partnership with PL — the nation's leader in specialty staffing for Accounting and Finance.

ABC, founded in 1942, is the world's largest labour and employment law firm. With more than 1,000 attorneys and over 60 offices spanning the globe, ABC has litigated and mediated some of the most historical employment cases and labor contracts on record.

PL is searching on a Director of Strategic Pricing for ABC in the greater Kansas City, MO area.

Director of Strategic Pricing Job Responsibilities:

- Ensure pricing strategy and pricing decisions reflect sound business judgment, alignment of client and firm interests, and preserve and protect the firm's assets
- Evaluate and improve processes to enhance service, save costs and drive efficiencies
- Leverage technology to improve strategic pricing analytics and data management
- Responsible for ensuring department policies and procedures are current and reflect best practice methods
- Handle inquiries from shareholders, clients, vendors and other third parties
- Ensure duties are appropriately distributed amongst team members
- Motivate, train, develop, provide feedback to and retain employees

Skills and Qualifications:

- Bachelor's degree in Accounting, Finance or related field
- Master's degree or advanced certification preferred
- Significant management experience in high volume, multi-location, multi-currency finance department
- Experience within a Law Firm or Professional Services Firm desired
- Proficiency in Excel and ability to work with large sets of complex data
- Ability to recruit, lead and mentor a fast paced team

If you are qualified and interested in learning more about this Director of Strategic Pricing job opportunity at ABC, please send your resume for immediate consideration. You can also view additional career openings.

Legal pricing – An Emerging Profession

Introductory paragraph - Article by Stephen Petrie
Published by Legal Solutions, Thomson Reuters

https://info.legalsolutions.thomsonreuters.com/signup/newsletters/practice-innovations/2013-oct/article4.aspx

In recent years, the legal industry has witnessed the advent and proliferation of professional pricing. Firms have inserted this growing administrative function into the organizational structure in a variety of different ways, often establishing these capabilities within Finance or Business Development and Marketing. As the Chief Strategy Officer for Faegre Baker Daniels, I oversee the pricing function within the Strategy & Operations department—yet another organisational alternative. The business professionals who perform this work go by many different titles and often wear multiple hats. While a variety of analytical responsibilities (e.g. profitability analysis) may be embedded in a pricing role, efficiency-related disciplines (e.g. legal process improvement and project management) are, far and away, the most common areas of overlap. This is logical, given the direct correlation that exists between efficiency and profitability when operating in a fixed-fee context.

Professional Pricing Society
wwwpricingsociety.com

There is even a 'society' dedicated to professional pricing. This organisation provides online training and even a certification process.

INTERESTED? NEXT STEPS

Invest in deepening your own knowledge in the area of pricing? You may not be about to hire a Pricing Director but you may agree that a profession without standard pricing needs to be professional and business like in its approach to the pricing of its services.

My response is to look at some basic steps that adhere to the principle of best billing practices.

Starting with...

1. Always hire the best. I have consulted with a number of firms who are suffering from having staff who they describe as perhaps *"not the best."*
2. Invest in training and staff reviews. If perhaps you do not tick the above box then do not restrain yourself from investing in training. Start with the firm owners and then establish programmes for each individual – including the person known as 'the receptionist.'

3. Every job should have a section devoted to *"What I need to do better next time"* and/or – *"this is where I need further help/training to do my job better."*
4. Training clients to deliver what is required when it is required.
5. Checking that you have what is required.
6. Planning jobs effectively. Fair targets. Allowing staff what is required to do the job. Good oversight while work is in progress including positive reinforcement where appropriate. Constructive review and appraisal.

MOVING ONTO

Time. Knowing what **time** it takes to do a minimum of 95 per cent of your routine compliance jobs. Staff should be aiming to deliver on target – or within 95 per cent.

Value. There is value in compliance but, like your car engine, it is just assumed. When you buy a car you tend to spend far more time looking at the interior and extras – not under the bonnet. The key is to deliver such outstanding value around the perimeter of your services that the client's mindset is one of complete satisfaction and assurance in a service well executed by a firm whose personnel are highly regarded.

Moving clients up from a focus on your cost to a focus on value and service and an acceptance of the cost.

There will always be firms who will say they will charge less and those who will charge more.

Avoid:

- Guessing
- The first job trap – remember that the first fee can so easily set the benchmark for future fees. Ensure that clients know you will revisit the price having completed the first year. That way you avoid having year on year job losses.
- Not addressing the client's failure to deliver good records

A FEW KEYS WHEN DISCUSSING PRICES WITH CLIENTS OR PROSPECTS

1. Have a process – and one that is inclusive. Use a collaborative pricing approach.
2. Use an average hourly rate - you should have calculated this after studying Chapter 2
3. Engage with the sign off of a second person

And finally, as this is a chapter on pricing directors – who is your best pricer in the firm? Why not appoint an internal 'pricing partner'. Invest in books on pricing such as Implementing Value Pricing (Ron Baker) and Smarter Pricing. Smarter Profits.

The key takeaway?

I suspect that appointing a pricing director is probably not on your list of action points, but there is a really valuable principle that we can apply - especially where there is more than one firm owner. But there is a key action point that we need to consider.

DO YOU HAVE A STANDARD LIST OF PRICES FOR ALL YOUR VARIOUS SERVICES?

Whether it is during my seminars or working as a consultant with accounting firms I often present myself as a prospective client. I provide as much information regarding my company as I am able and then ask those in attendance to ask any questions they wish before I then ask them for a quote for their services. It maybe the audit or just the compilation and tax service. The results? The difference between the lowest and highest is usually about 250% - often more. Interesting as it tells us what we already know and that is that there is [currently] no standard price for our compliance services. The price is what a willing professional is happy to charge and a client willing to pay. Rates vary from one provider to another - that is the way it has always been – but maybe not the way it will be in the future.

This price variation is almost certain to prevail in your firm - one person will quote a different price for the same basic service when compared to another. The likelihood is that the one who quotes the higher price may well recover all or most of the time while the lower price will almost certainly result in time write off – any may be unhappy staff and even an unhappy client.

HERE IS WHAT TO DO TO AT LEAST BE ON THE SAME PAGE

Determine the range of your basic services and develop an internal benchmark as to what the lowest fee is and the range of fees for a particular type of service.

I know some firms who have done this and find their internal document an essential practice management tool.

The future?

I think that price transparency is inevitable and it may be a better approach than the current one if you are billing last year's fee plus inflation.

THE EMERGING ROLE OF THE PRICE DIRECTOR | 17

QUESTIONS TO ASK YOURSELF

1

What are your prices for your regularly recurring services?

2

What will you do to ensure that all those involved in pricing at least take serious note of these prices?

3

Do you know what your firm's average realised billing rate is?

> **PRICE** IS WHAT YOU **PAY**. **VALUE** IS WHAT YOU **GET**.
>
> **WARREN BUFFETT**

18 DOWNSIZE YOUR LOCK UP

Unbilled work is still an inevitable aspect of standard practice throughout the profession. Similarly outstanding debtors (receivables) feature in almost all firms' current assets. Added together (including the value of unbilled work at 'sale value' the combined total is often referred to as 'lock up'. In the 30 or so years I have been around observing the profession as a consultant it has been a common feature to see firm balance sheets and inter firm surveys routinely showing lock up of between 25-35 per cent [of gross fees net of sales tax]. Sometimes even more. As accountants we view lock up as an asset. But is it?

In 2008 a new term entered the world's financial lexicon: toxic debt. It was the term used to describe the pile of debt incurred by bad [reckless] bank lending.

Shortly after the 'global financial crisis' Richard Sergeant, the managing director of PracticeWEB, adapted the phrase in reference to lock up, he called it 'toxic lock up.'

The use of this phrase often illicits a wry smile at seminars. However, there is more, much more to this than it simply being a neat phrase.

THE DETRIMENTAL EFFECT OF TOXIC LOCK UP

It is I believe close to being a fact that if you were to compile an inter firm survey, the average lock up of the 500,000 or so global accounting firms would probably be somewhere in the region of between 25 to 35 per cent. But, never mind other firms, what about yours? If the answer to the question is over 15 per cent let me share with you what I realised when asking myself what the effect of 'toxic lock up' really is.

In my view there are two serious, adverse consequences of excessive lock up. These are both serious and adverse – and may even be a primary reason why so many accounting firms do not succeed in doing more than compliance work for clients.

EFFECT NUMBER ONE

Imagine a client whose financial statements are nearing completion. Unless they have been sent an interim account which has been paid it is likely that your job lock up at this juncture is at a peak. It is not every practitioner that at this point feels a compelling surge of selling prowess to interest the client in further services. That is especially true if the client has a slow payment history. The reality is that lock up acts as a restraint both consciously and subconsciously to your engaging with the client about any significant additional service.

If the job is nearing completion and recovery is heading for 90 per cent or less, your motivation is primarily driven by the desire to finish the job, send out the invoice and get paid.

EFFECT NUMBER TWO

Your client is in the same situation as you but sees reality from their perspective. They know you are about to complete the work and send out accounts together with an invoice for the work performed. They also know it will probably take a couple of months before pressure is applied to pay. So, in this situation the client probably does not feel it appropriate to extend the debt further.

Thus, you do not feel you can sell additional service and the client does not feel they can buy any further service.

That is the double whammy of toxic lock up!

KNOWN OR UNKNOWN?

In order to build high impact professional relationships it is important to provide a service where the client is being made aware of those things which are unknown.

Let's look at this from the perspective of a visit to the doctor.... You have during the last few days been sneezing, probably for the first couple of days you didn't bother to take any medication thinking that your ailment will surely pass. But the sneezing, aches and headaches continue. You are finally persuaded to head for the doctors and while there you are informed, not unexpectedly, that you have influenza. You thank the doctor for the prescription and the diagnosis and leave heading for the pharmacy. How did the visit rate? It was just what you expected – nothing unexpected, no real surprise! This was all **known** information - you probably knew you had the flu!

Now another scenario.... You feel a few chest pains which persist more than you expect and maybe you respond a little more quickly to making an appointment to see the doctor. The doctor, asks a few questions, takes your blood pressure, she looks a little concerned before announcing that you are to be referred to a hospital heart consultant. *"I will see how quickly I can get an appointment for you,"* she says.

Now the diagnosis of the doctor and the action she is advising are taking you into the unknown and by the time you meet the consultant you are ready to answer questions, listen and ensure you understand what the problem is and what your options are to fully recover.

I liken the first scenario to our compliance work where the outcomes are generally known in advance. In the second scenario you are entering **unknown** territory and you may have been wondering if your symptoms are life-threatening.

HOW DOES THIS COMPARE WITH YOUR SERVICES AND YOUR PROFESSIONAL EXPERTISE?

When you prepare financial statements it could well be that you:

Confirm the results the client was expecting – the client had looked at the trial balance results from their computer systems and had concluded that they were about 10 per cent up on the previous year. The fact that you reported profit was up by 12 per cent was not overly material to the client.

You calculate the tax which the client had already estimated would be last year's tax bill plus tax at the higher rate on the additional 10 per cent profit. So, maybe the client underestimated a little.

So, the **unknowns** we used to hold sway over are not really **unknowns** anymore.

However, the client is interested to find out how much your fee is!

The client now has an anchor in his/her mind that your service revolves around confirming what they know and that the work you perform relates to times gone by rather than the future.

I do not seek to downgrade the value of your services, merely to provide an alternative perspective.

The reality is that most firms do not generate more than 10 per cent of their fees from non-compliance services. Those firms that do probably have specialists operating in areas other than compliance work. But it is these services where you are exploring more unknown areas, where potentially there is greater pain and greater value in addressing the pain.

> **Key Point:** High impact professional relationships are ALWAYS predicated on the unknown. Your additional services are an opportunity to explore the unknowns thus creating greater value.

THE CONCLUSION

In this, the first of two chapters on billing and collections we have looked at the negative impact of lock up and the fact that so much of what the accountant delivers today is relatively known or suspected. We [thankfully] do not often bring unexpected or unpleasant information to the client's attention. Like the doctor and the flu diagnosis – compliance work usually delivers the **known**.

However, taking the example of the heart consultant here we see the impact and power of the **unknown**.

If almost every chapter of this book makes reference to your additional service portfolio it is because ultimately compliance services, the bedrock of an accountancy firm's business thus far, are withering on the vine. Not to disappear forever but services with clients ever price conscious against a background of technology creep and changing approaches by governments to the supply of the information they require to collect taxes.

Toxic lock up restricts your ability to super serve the client. So, is there an answer? Read on.

QUESTIONS TO ASK YOURSELF

By how much do you plan to reduce our lock up?

What strategies will you employ?

Who is responsible for implementation and for ensuring that these processes do not fall by the wayside?

> **PLANS** ARE ONLY **GOOD INTENTIONS** UNLESS THEY IMMEDIATELY **DEGENERATE** INTO HARD **WORK**.
>
> PETER DRUCKER

19 NEW BILLING AND COLLECTING HORIZONS FOR TODAY

In 2013 the closure was announced of hundreds of retail shops along with the initial loss of thousands of UK jobs by Comet (electrical retailer), HMV (record shop), and Jessops (cameras). Round about the same time Blockbuster closed a large number of its UK stores. Thankfully HMV and Jessops subsequently reopened with new owners injecting fresh capital and with a greater investment and understanding of the electronic marketplace.

At the beginning of 2013 Amazon announced their pre-Christmas sales had increased by one third to £1.4 billion. Of course, many of the goods sold by these closed stores are available from Amazon which long ago ceased to be just a bookseller.

But the reasons behind the closure of HMV included a failure to recognise the changing marketplace with more businesses now offering downloadable products as opposed to physical ones. Further so many goods can now be ordered online and delivered to your door.

The question this provokes is *"what do changes in technology mean for the accounting profession."* And, if there are implications, what are they and what should be done?

Well, we know that no one knows what the future holds. But, notwithstanding that obvious statement, let me detail some changes that I perceive as [welcome, as well as] inevitable.

CHANGE WILL COME

I recall listening to President Obama during his 2012 re-election campaign. He had four years earlier promised the American people change – in fact it was his resonating offer of change that was a major contributory reason for his election in 2008. Four years later many felt that change had failed to materialise and so he changed his proposition to say that *"change is on the way."* The thoughts and ideas I share are not based on what is happening in accounting but out in the global marketplace. Much has and is changing in the way we do business, yet there hasn't necessarily been much significant change in the profession. But there are a good number of firms who are already doing some of the things I am now going to discuss.

ARE YOU LOOKING TO INCREASE YOUR OWN INVESTMENT IN THE BUSINESS?

The good news is that some firms are seeing significant increases in profitability with firm owners retaining less of their own capital in the business. In so doing they are generally gaining high levels of client approval. But, before we go further allow me to address one major issue: it is going to be easy for you to read what I write but think it is impossible for you to make any change. These are the 'things are okay as they are' and 'my clients will not go for that' syndromes. Well, what if I suggest to you that this approach results in locking yourself into delivering a lower level of service compared to other more entrepreneurial firms? Furthermore, are you content allowing yourself to continue with the level of lock up that you have today – and if nothing changes, what will it look like tomorrow? How much more capital [retained profit] will you need to leave in the business? Finally, how much of your capital is invested in the business? If you had the chance to draw some of this out – would you say *"no, I don't really need it?!"*

RATING AUTHORITIES AND UTILITY COMPANIES INTRODUCE CHANGE

Many years ago local authorities in the UK used to collect household rates every six months. Today most of us pay by 10 instalments a year with two 'free months' in February and March – now hold that for a short while as I will revisit this later on.

Similarly, utility companies used to request payment at the end of every quarter whereas today the majority of households use the direct debt payment system with a periodic adjustment for underpayment or a refund if there is an overpayment – and again – hold this for a short while as I paint the picture of future change.

CAN YOU RECALL ALL THOSE CREDITOR SCHEDULES YOU HAVE PREPARED OR REVIEWED?

I'd like you to do something I have asked hundreds of accountants to do in my seminars – that is to recall every creditor schedule you have ever prepared or reviewed. Having done that, I'd like you to think about this question *"which was the last creditor to be paid?"* Without asking you to pursue this question too long, is it not the accountancy bill that is the last account the client pays?

What is the lesson here? Maybe it is that our business clients are accustomed to paying for goods and services in the year to which those goods and services relate – give or take 30/60 days. So, on what basis do we accountants think it is appropriate to step outside clients' normal standard business practices?

Okay, I know what you are thinking, but stop looking at your current billing practices - the way you have [always] done billing and look at the new world in which standard business practices have evolved.

As we establish some basic principles I am going to ask you to keep hold of this one as well.

> *"Billing is one of the most important skills in the successful practice of a profession. To be financially successful you must learn to bill more for those engagements that justify a higher fee while at the same time protecting client relationships from price competition."*
> **David W. Cottle, David Cottle Consulting, USA**

FINALLY, THE POINTS COME TOGETHER

My next and, you will be pleased to read, final point is to ask this question...

"What have you bought in the last year for which you did not know in advance the cost?"

Probably very few transactions come to mind. When you commit to a purchase you almost certainly commit to a known cost. Now, with the Internet increasingly the source of many billions of transactions, can you find a website where a cost is not specified with a required payment up front before any transaction can be completed? We transact in advance of supply with companies we have never heard of and we probably do no research on their credit or trustworthiness.

My point? Is that the world has dramatically changed its business practices as a result of the revolution in technology and the capability of the Internet.

ACCOUNTANTS SUBSCRIBING TO KARL MARX?

The time cost basis of billing clients is the one that was accepted throughout the 20th century. Did you know that it has its origins in the works of Karl Marx? Marx together with Friedrich Engels was the co-author of The Communist Manifesto, a manifesto which still wields considerable power and influence over some of the world's countries and even over the pricing of professional firm services! His ideology is so deeply ingrained into our value paradigm that we do not notice it, let alone subject ourselves to considering its validity.

Marx gave us a definition of value that is so deeply ingrained in the profession's approach to pricing that it has to be time for it to be challenged.

Marx explained his labour theory of value in Value, Price and Profit published in 1865.

"A commodity has a value, because it is a crystallisation of social labour. The greatness of its value, or its relative value, depends upon the greater or less amount of that social substance contained in it; that is to say, on the relative mass of labour necessary for its production. The relative values of commodities are, therefore, determined by the respective quantities or amounts of labour, worked up, realised, fixed in them. The correlative quantities of commodities which can be produced in the same time of labour are equal." Marx, 1995:31.

If that theory were correct then a stone taken out of a mine would have the same value as a diamond found next to it. So, maybe it is time to look again at the billable hour?

HOW LONG DID IT TAKE...

- To manufacture the car you drive?
- To build the home you live in?
- To make the clothes you wear?
- To print the magazine you read?
- How much does it cost the provider to send your text message?

The reality is you probably don't know the answer to those questions, and you probably don't care!

Could there be any similarity between your answer to those questions and your client's attitude toward your fees?

> *"If accountants don't value their time or work, neither will their clients."*
> **David W. Cottle, David Cottle Consulting, USA**

THE CONSUMER HAS ALREADY MADE THE CHANGE

Let us hone in on an approach to cost/price that I believe has already taken place in the mindset of the consumer of professional services, and in reality also in the mind of many accountants. It is possible however that, while some action has already been taken, this has been to a large extent in response to feedback from clients. For example, if a client complains about the level of the fee it is common to seek to accommodate the client who has the boldness to complain and in so doing maybe even agree the price for the forthcoming year. I know it has always been like this, but now we are looking at what I believe will become standard practice. So why not take the leap and get ahead.

YOUR FEES FOR THE LAST 12 MONTHS ARE A POWERFUL ANCHOR

I have one final proposition for you and it is this: if I was to look at your firm's invoices for the last 12 months, I would reckon that, apart from maybe five per cent of invoices, your fees for each client for the next year, give or take a per cent or two, will probably be based on last year's fee adjusted for the current rate of inflation. Yes, there may be one or two extra costs for additional work, but the core compliance fee will be determined by last year's fee. I call this being subject to the 'law of anchoring' where the amount of the previous year's fee manages the client's expectation of what the accountant's future costs will be. In other words everyone is working to a price for services rendered that is relatively fixed. Fixed, even though this year's work is almost certainly going to be different from last year's work.

You know that's just the way it works – most are unwilling to approach a client about client-caused problems at the time they arise and by the time the bill is prepared it looks even clearer that the additional time is going to have to be absorbed – maybe not for the first time.

WHAT PICTURE ARE WE LOOKING AT?

Let me bring all the pieces of the jigsaw together and the points I have been making and see if we can paint a clear picture.

At this moment in time I know of no country where a consumer of professional services can go online and do a price comparison or find a standard price list. Sometime in the future, what I have suggested will become out of date and prices for certain standard services will be routinely quoted on websites. At the time of writing I know of a few websites where you can enter basic details of your accounting and tax requirements together with certain base data and be given a fixed fee. Just think of Expedia, Opodo or Ebookers and you will see my point. With Expedia and other similar sites you enter four or five selection criteria and after submitting this information you are offered a series of options from which you then select. What is to stop someone creating a similar platform in the accountancy marketplace or indeed firms themselves creating such a model for their website? Possible? I think so.

GOOD NEWS

Feeling 'unsettled' by all of this? Wait, there is a lot of good news in all of this so let me continue. The approach I am going to share with you has enabled many firms to virtually eliminate their lock up and improve profits while at the same time enhancing client relationships.

I think this is probably one of the biggest challenges and probably the single biggest leap for many firms, but you need to know that others have already done this and many more will follow. I call this approach the 'we're not our clients' bankers any longer!' This will make your firm financially leaner and have clients welcoming your newly honed pricing and collection practice.

Let me outline a series of steps you need to take. From this you will then be able to determine your own approach.

Step 1:

Fix your price. This will be for the regular work that recurs from one year to the next. This will probably be closely linked to the price charged for the same work undertaken in the last year unless you have consistently incurred significant write downs and need to negotiate a fairer price.

Step 2:

Your proposal to the client. The client is going to be pleased to able to discuss and agree a price with you – after all that brings you into line with every other supplier they deal with.

Step 3:

And the real key is that this is a win-win for you and your client.

Remember that, in theory at least, the cost plus billing system has at its root the intention that you should be paid for every hour – regardless of how efficient, effective or honest you are with your time recording. Therefore the cost-risk is borne by the client with the consequence that they will seek to manage your time and be careful about incurring more time cost. However, when you agree a fee up front with the client the risk is reversed – and of course, this risk needs to be managed.

Step 4:

Prepare your documentation. Standard letters may help in confirming what has been agreed with your client. I recommend discussing this face-to-face with clients. If you send out a standard letter only a few clients will respond.

Step 5:

Fine-tune the financial proposal. Herein lays the challenge. Because you have been billing in arrears the hurdle you have to jump over involves catch up.

Now, the quantum of the catch up depends on how much the client owes, how much is to be billed and the extent to which the client is through the current accounting period. So, you will probably wish to phase this in with clients over a 12 month period catching them as soon as you can after the financial year end.

HERE ARE A RANGE OF SOLUTIONS

Client with year end 31 December. Owes £1,200 in unpaid bills. Proposed fee for the next 12 months is £2,400. Meeting with the client in March when there is a further £1,800 to be paid. So, one point to make is that this is not a system or approach for clients to pay off arrears. So, the client needs to pay the firm £3,000 – that is in the normal course of the financial relationship. Let's assume that this is paid by 31 May. When it is paid is almost irrelevant because payment should be made by that date. Then from 1 June the client is asked to pay £240 a month for the ten months to the end of March – by which time you will be completing their work for the year.

Client with year end 31 December. Just about to have work undertaken for £2,100. Proposed fee for the next 12 months is £2,100. So here we are looking to have the client pay £4,200. They are going to pay that – the only question to be resolved is when. Options: Client could pay you as normal or you could offer to have a direct debit set up for, say, three payments of £700 followed by 10 payments of £210.

MY PREFERRED SOLUTION LOOKS LIKE THIS…

Meet with all clients three months before their financial year end and explain your new financial policy/practice. Have them sign a direct debit form. The first six payments will cover the cost for the forthcoming annual work. Thus if your fee is agreed at £1,200 then there will be six payments of £200. Following these payments the client can then either continue with payments for the next year, or have a two month break.

> If the former approach is agreed: Your client will be debited in the fourth month of their year for 1/12th i.e. £100.

> If the latter, opting for the two free months, then in the sixth month a series of 10 £120 payments will commence.

In both instances the last payment will be processed a few months after the client's year end when you will be completing your annual work.

Step 6:

Meet with your client. Remember all you are asking the client to agree to is a payment plan that is consistent with how they pay for their other goods and services. Have them sign the direct debit. Agree the arrangements and then follow through with a letter.

A FEW OBSERVATIONS AND OBJECTIONS

"Our clients won't agree?" Who says so? Have you asked them – or are you verbalising your unwillingness to offer clients a better service? Furthermore,

whose business is it? Surely it is for you, the supplier to table your payment arrangements. Is paying 12 months after work was done (you may have billed in March but some of that work might go back to April 11 months prior) a good business practice?

"We use standing orders." Yes, so did I once upon a time twenty five years ago! Big mistake as every time you wish to increase the order there is one further opportunity to have a discussion about payment arrangements.

"Not all clients will agree to the change." But surely we don't manage our business to the lowest common denominator? Or, if we do – maybe out of fear of lost clients or upsetting clients…. Remember it is your business.

GETTING TOUGH

Take a look at what is in your 90 day columns (WIP and debtors). What is the combined value and what is this as a percentage of your gross income? Whatever the answer, the quantum is likely to be too high. That is 'income' you would have liked in your bank a long time ago. To follow through with this strategy requires toughness. Keep in mind it is your business, you are giving a world class service and you need to be paid. You are not there as investors in your client's business.

A WIN-WIN SITUATION

Here is one compelling reason to adopt this system of payment. I believe that the existence of lock up is a major inhibitor to the delivery of further services – for the two reasons mentioned in the last chapter:

You as the provider of the service wish to be paid for the work that has already been billed and is unpaid as well as for the WIP currently standing in the cost records. Therefore, offering your client a further service before being paid is unlikely to be high on your agenda. Yes, you could offer any further service on condition of the account being brought up-to-date – that is standard practice for some, but nevertheless adds a complication to the discussions with the client.

Similarly, the client knows that money is owed and also recognises that a further account may well be winging its way shortly. Clients, being mostly honourable people, are unlikely to wish to rush into requesting further work until the existing financial obligation is clear.

Having your ongoing annual fees paid by direct debit removes this complication from the decision to undertake any further work.

A compelling result for you and the firm.

Often 90 per cent or more of the capital invested in an accounting business is funding lock up. In fact, if you were to liquidate lock up the balance sheet would have a surplus of cash almost equivalent to the capital invested by the firm owners. As my American friends say *"do the math."*

How would you feel if you were to go home and ask your spouse/significant other how they would feel if you could bank 50 per cent of the balance on your capital account? I say no more!

AND FINALLY... A SELECTION OF TERMS AND CONDITIONS

When a fee is agreed in advance the risk is assumed by you the provider. It is therefore incumbent on you to manage that risk. Start by sending out a pre year end checklist detailing the records required for your work to commence AND a date by when these records should be delivered.

Here are a few possible 'standard' conditions:

1. All control accounts to be balanced
2. Completeness of records
3. Prompt response to queries
4. There may need to be a review if your top line varies by more than x%

You should also let clients know who is working on their records and the fact they may / will make contact for further information

> **Key point:** Do not fail to adopt this for new clients for whom time billing makes little sense. This would be a missed opportunity of gigantic proportions.

QUESTIONS TO ASK YOURSELF

1
How persuaded are you to introduce changes to your billing practices?

2
What can you to do move on from 20th century billing practices?

3
Your plan. Who is going to do what and by when?

> **BILL YOUR CLIENTS WHILE THE TEARS OF APPRECIATION ARE MOIST IN THEIR EYES.**
>
> DAVE COTTLE — AT LEAST I FIRST HEARD HIM USE THIS IN A SEMINAR IN THE 1980s

20 | POWER UP YOUR GROSS MARGIN

INTRODUCTION

There are only two ways to improve your margin - you can either increase the price you charge or reduce the cost of delivering the service – or both of course! This chapter aims to look at how you can improve your planning, your quoting and reducing the time cost of client work.

Let's start with a couple of job costing approaches:

How do you establish the time cost of doing the work? There are numerous approaches, the main ones include using software, using the previous year's fee as a benchmark or sitting down and seeking to calculate the time to do the job or value pricing.

I think that value pricing is undoubtedly where the marketplace is heading but I do believe that we should understand how long it will take or has taken to do the job.

One approach I employed while in practice was the 'client budgeting form.' This enables me to go through one by one all the various components of the work the client needs us to perform, understand the financial quantum we are dealing with and agreeing with the client the budgeted time to complete the work. You will see that for each entry there is a minimum time requirement. This approach enabled me to observe that, *"I am sure we can complete that in the minimum time"* where this was appropriate.

Having compiled all the hours you will see there is a blank when it comes to the average rate per hour. What value do you include here? Here is a range of options:

1. Establish your average staff rate at *charge rate value* for performing this type of work, or
2. Establish the *historical realised rate* for performing this type of work.

In practice this value gives you the ability to determine the budgeted time cost that requires investing. Maybe there is an element of flexibility in the hourly value you opt to include?

It is also important to discuss with the client what additional services they require, e.g. taxation, management accounts, management meetings etc.

So, when you have established the time cost (aided of course by your client) you can move to propose/agree the fee. If the client thinks it is too high do not *automatically* reduce the cost. Maybe look at what additional work the client could perform on the records to reduce the time. Maybe there are some services they might decide not to initially opt for? It is important to resist the emotion of fear – fear of not winning the business.

This approach involves one of openness and collaboration instead of plucking a figure out of the air, using your best judgment which might not be as reliable as you think. Worse or quoting just less than the previous accountant charged.

\multicolumn{5}{l	}{CLIENT BUDGETING – UP TO £X MILLION}
SECTION	WORK TO DO	VALUE	COMMENT	MIN HRS	HOURS
A	Accounts – Trial Balance			15	
B	Analytical Review			5	
C	Planning			4	
D	Points for Review			3	
E	Fixed assets			8	
F	Expenditure/Creditors			15	
G	Directors/Partners			10	
H	Stock/WIP			15	
I	Revenue/Debtors			15	
J	Cash and Bank			6	
K	Taxation			10	
L	Share Capital			2	
M	Journals			5	
N	Detailed Nominal			20	
Other	Accounting work				
	Total hours				
	Average cost @ £____p.h.				£
					£

	Partner review			600	
	Client business and management advice			800	
	Company taxation			500	
	Expenses			0	
	Personal taxation			600	
	Budgeted time costs				£
	Agreed fee				£
	Initial meetings and file set up				£

LET'S LOOK NOW AT THREE MORE IMPORTANT BUDGETING LESSONS:

Lesson 1

Ensure that when managers produce budgets they budget what it takes to do the job. Firm owners should not put staff under pressure to reduce the budget down to the fee you believe the job can be billed for. That only serves to put unrealistic pressure on the manager and may lead to inappropriate short cuts, or more commonly a productivity variance. A better approach is for the manager to be given the time necessary to do the job and then hold them to account for delivering the job according to their budget. This means the manager owns the budget and consequently connects with the responsibility to do everything possible to deliver within budget.

There seems to be a manager gene that results in managers being optimistic budgeters – a gene that needs to be addressed. Stress the importance of doing it right and fully anticipating the time commitment.

Lesson 2

This concerns collating critical feedback from the staff when the job is completed. Imagine you have just completed a job – if you were to start the job again – would you take less time? I have never heard anyone say *"No"* in response to this question. Of course you could do it in less time. So, learning from these job experiences I believe best practice is for staff to pass important information about critical processes on from one year to the next. This is information that is deemed mission-critical when it comes to the manager briefing staff next time around. Why not prepare an outline budget for next year's job at the conclusion of this year's work? I achieve this feedback by using a form I call the *'job postscript'* a copy of which follows. You can also download from my website at marklloydbottom.com.

1. The first part of this form asks the manager or senior to list out just three things next year's senior needs to know to succeed on the job. It may be quite simple – turn up on time – or don't leave the bank statements out!

2. The next step is to identify the three things next year's senior should do to reduce this year's elapsed time. It could be phone up a week before the job is due to start and make sure they have those specified documents or reconciliations ready. This form need not be too wordy – it needs to capture the key lessons learnt. It must not turn out to be a dissertation!

3. Then the last section of the form is for the senior on the job to concisely summarise why the job did not meet budget this time around – if that is the case.

JOB POSTSCRIPT

Client: _____ P/E _____

Prepared By: _____ On: _____

For Next Year's A.I.C.

These are the three keys you need to know to succeed on this job:

1	*Always arrive early** *The points included are for illustrative purposes only
2	*Do not waste time chatting with staff*
3	*Ask for M.D.'s accounts*

	These are the three keys you need to know to beat the time elapsed on this year's job
1	*Make sure client keeps supplier's statements*
2	*Watch for client caused problems in sales ledger*
3	*Don't waste time trying to balance the purchase control*
	I wish you every success

Lesson 3

Negotiate fees early. From my experience most budgets are prepared so close to the start of the job they do not allow any time for any fee-focused conversation with the client. Imagine calling a client a week before the job is due to start and seeking to increase the price by 15% compared to the previous year. That sounds like putting the client's back against the wall, and possibly they are on their way to becoming an ex client anyway!

So, I recommend the first draft of the budget is prepared immediately after the job has been completed so this gives you the best part of 40+ weeks to bring the matter of fees and your level of work to the client's attention. Perhaps the client's staff could do more work in advance of your work commencing?

Maybe it is just me but when I was lead partner jobs always ended up on my desk with no time left for my own work – I never found that a great motivator! From this problem I developed a solution that I call the 'decreasing budget' – there are several action components to this so let me start at the beginning.

THE DECREASING BUDGET

Take a job with an elapsed time cost of £11,800 and a fee of £9,000 – therefore total time written off of £2,800. The time before the job started was £800, the job took £9,000 worth of time and the partner review and meeting time cost £2,000. My question is which £2,800 is written off?

The fact is, we can't tell. Does that scenario sound familiar? So let's look at each of the three components of the time.

1 Bill the time on before the job starts

The manager might contend the time on the job before the main work commenced was time that was 'dumped' there – not representing anything of real billable value.

The firm owner would no doubt contend this is high quality time in which he gave amazing advice at some really impactful meetings with the client.

So, let's make sure it is not this £800 that is written off. So partner – this sounds like great work so bill it before the job starts. To which the partner agrees and bills it for £1,000 thus leaving a £200 profit to go against the main job.

2 Ring fence the time budget for the partner

Now let's go to the budgeted time for the partner at the end of the job. Well, we know this is dynamic and high value time so we are going to ask the manager to ring fence the £2,000 so that, whatever happens this budget remains intact for the partner to do partner stuff. File review and sign off, meeting preparation and attendance complete with some suggestions for other services deemed relevant to the client. So this is all high value and not time to be written off.

3 Is this where the write off lies?

Which means the only time that could be responsible for the write down is the time to do the job? Now, just bear with me because I am going to share some insights intended to help managers and seniors deliver the job on budget. Your time systems are adept at accumulating time. However, imagine if alternatively, the manager started off with £9,000 and then each week depreciated the elapsed job time so after week one there was a remaining budget of £6,000 and after two weeks the remaining balance was £2,500. Then the manager knows the job has to be completed if the job is not to incur a write down. Remember managers have been given the budget they prepared and all we ask is that they manage the work within budget. So, everyone is focused on making budget and on the lookout for genuine client-caused billable problems.

OK, so maybe you detect a little bias toward firm owners but the fact is productivity variances do arise because WIP is not billed before, what I call, the 'fog of the job' descends – when the earlier work performed and its value dims into the recesses of the client's mind. The partner's attitude can be, *"Oh, that will be included in the interim account when we are preparing the accounts."* Decreasing the budget sharpens everyone's focus and the partner investing time on the job sign off also provides opportunity to look at other areas where we can be of value to the client.

EXTRAS OR UNFORESEEN WORK

The challenge of how to address charging for extras has long vexed accounting firm owners. Do you call the client and invite them to have the records back to fix the problem? Sounds like good advice but you are unlikely to hear a thank you from the client for returning the books they have been meaning to bring in to the office for weeks. Neither do you wish to wait for the records to come back in. So, many default to fixing the problem and then seeing what level of charge the client may accept when the costs are being discussed. This is perhaps the most common approach because, in reality, it is the one that gives rise to the least problem with client communication. But, the result very often is increased and unrecovered time costs.

Is there another way? And, of course the answer is a resounding 'yes.'

The answer lies in looking at what accepted practices exist in other businesses. Let's take the car service reception as an example. You drop your car off at 8.30am and then at precisely 9.27am you receive a call – it is the call that you hoped not to hear. *"Service have looked at the car and have reported back that there are a few areas that need attention…"* You listen and then ask, *"What is the cost?"* And of course the caller has standard costs ready and waiting for you to eventually say, *"Yes, do carry on."*

It is a powerful lesson on how to address the question of faults or extra time costs. So how can an accounting firm adopt this principle given that this is, to a large extent, an accepted approach to extras?

First step: Determine the main areas where client-caused problems arise

Second step: Establish how long it typically takes to fix the problem

Third step: Like the garage – contact the client and communicate clearly the cost of the fix. In this area it is essential to avoid the time elapsed approach. If you feel unable to adopt one price for balancing a bank account then develop a range. The key is to be upfront with the client and gain their early acknowledgement and agreement to you fixing the problem.

MY CASEBOOK

Let's look at some management lessons I have learnt from managers when seeking to explain the reasons for time over and above budget. Before

I start, let me say the vast majority of managers I have interviewed have expressed frustration that jobs run over budget. So this manager feedback comes with recommendations regarding what needs to be done differently in order to avoid exceeding budget. I record what manager's have said to me while consulting on improving firm profitability. So, these case studies are presented in the form of a conversation between me and Julian one of the managers I worked with.

Julian - please tell me what managers are saying about problems that arise in making budget and then I will make some suggestions to see how we can address the challenge you have raised.

> *"Yes Mark – well we find there are so many pre job checklists that budgeting is but one of a range of forms we need to complete and all of our planning has to be completed within three to four hours."*

Julian I understand that job planning is time consuming and covers a wide range of areas. However, permit me to emphasise that job budgeting is one of your most important pre job tasks. While there are many forms to be completed this section in particular is really important as it addresses such areas as the allocation of our staff and our ability to recover the time expended on the job. We need to make sure we have taken on board the lessons from last year's job as well as applying the lessons we have learnt around the office in the past year. It is our aim to have managers provide a budget that is at least 95 per cent accurate so the partner knows what, if any, the sales variance is. It's the partner's responsibility to do what can be done to maximise the fee. Accuracy in budgeting is of essential importance from the beginning to the end of the job. So, please do all you can to craft a budget that staff will respect as being realistic and seek to keep to it.

> *"Interesting Mark, thanks. I find there is excessive time on a number of jobs because some of the staff spent time doing things they shouldn't, maybe due to their inexperience."*

Well, we should remember staff's charge rate reflects their level of experience and expertise, but I do understand that on-the-job training needs will arise. In this instance I would suggest you have staff charge time (which managers need to approve) to a training section on the client's cost records and then at the end of every month assess all the arising needs and run training sessions to ensure next time the right procedures are followed. With all your systems the key to ongoing success is ensuring staff know what to do. Ensure that firm-wide you learn from all the jobs and see where the firm's systems and processes need to improve. Otherwise you are going to find these problems will keep recurring.

> **"Some of my staff have had to spend time balancing control accounts which was not planned for."**

Before the job starts, maybe a week or two in advance, it should be standard procedure to ask clients to confirm they have reconciliations for the bank, purchase, sales and any other important control accounts. Or, if the firm is to be responsible, then ensure the client accepts this will incur an additional charge. Unlike most other trades we fear to use the word 'extra' – it is as if the word does not exist in the accountants' lexicon. If the firm is to be responsible for this work, rather than the client, ensure the client knows this work will be completed for a price. One approach that reduces the cost of this type of work is to employ an internal bookkeeper to undertake this reconciliation. They will probably have a lower charge rate than the main accounting or audit staff and this work could be completed before the audit or accounts team start their work. This work can then be charged separately as soon as the reconciliation work is complete.

"Sometimes problems arose we did not anticipate."

Isn't that nearly always the case. Julian, I have two observations here – first, I find managers almost all tend to be optimistic budgeters – an assumption is routinely made that the job will go according to plan. Often, not enough time is allocated to the time necessary to respond to manager and partner reviews. Sometimes I find that not enough time is budgeted for dealing with the special problems that arise with groups of companies and inter-company adjustments. We all understand that the reality nearly always differs from the planning assumptions and such difference can be significant. When I take my car in for a service, I normally receive a call within two or three hours advising me regarding some extra work that is required. This happens because the garage has a standard practice to contact the customer and gain approval for extra work. When I last engaged a builder on a home extension we asked for extra work and were quoted and billed for every single piece of additional work. The builder, like the garage owner, has a standard practice of agreeing and charging for extra work. But as accountants we tend to do the work first and then think about the fee later. We shy away from using the word 'extra' – why? Maybe for fear that any extra cost might drive the client away.

When my son was training to be a chartered accountant, his manager phoned him up almost every day and during the conversation asked if there were any 'client-caused' problems. While on site doing work he knew that he was accountable for doing his part to bring the job in on budget.

So, the key with this is to have good client communications and to manage client expectations and let them know they will be billed for extra work. Now, I am not suggesting you nickel and dime the client every time, but if there is additional work to be taken into account – the best and, frankly, only time to discuss this is when the problem arises – then at least the client has the option of fixing the problem themselves. Leave the billing until after the job is completed, and more than likely, this time will end up being part of the productivity variance.

My final recommend on this point is for managers to include time in the budget for the unforeseen. Yes, that may increase the difference between the budget and the anticipated budget but what we are seeking to do is to institutionalise accurate budgeting so budgets become 95 per cent or more reliable.

> *"We have two jobs where the fee for the management accounts has not been increased for four years."*

Well this looks as though the firm owner is wantonly eroding the job margin, accepting less for the job as each year passes and I can see margin is inevitably reducing.

Let me approach this by looking at a recommend that applies to all work. Firm owners' should agree each year the minimum increase billers should add to the fee compared to the previous year. Now, I know an increase cannot always be charged in every situation but at least agree a standard target percentage increase. I know a number of firms where at the annual retreat partners are asked to sign undertakings to adopt the decisions of the firm's management executive, including the minimum fee increase. Now, you're thinking this might not work for you? So you are happy to see your profitability decline are you? It's OK, on some occasions to break a rule – but it is important to have a rule for everyone to follow in the first instance.

> *"When we go through the cost records we find ad hoc work has been 'dumped' into audit."*

Oh, don't you just love that. Remember the tax exercise you performed - it was just a time dump! Well, let me make a really important point here. I find some firms have no more than one client cost account while others have multiple cost centres – each of these approaches presents a different challenge.

Where only one cost centre is used, there is always the likelihood one off work will be lost in the general client work and either not billed or under billed. However, where multiple cost centres are opened at will and when you look through the make-up of a client's accumulated time cost you find time has been charged to aborted projects or ones that have just simply gone nowhere and lapsed. I know it is sometimes almost impossible to tell if a client enquiry or initial conversation is going to convert into billable time that represents value to the client but you should introduce a standard policy of at least billing or writing off time either one or two months after the cost centre was opened or, alternatively, have a detailed review of all this type of work at the end of each calendar quarter. Fail to do this and you are unlikely to ever fully bill this time.

> *"I often have problems with staff being unavailable to complete work after I have completed my review because they are off on another job."*

The problem you refer to is what happens when staff are scheduled wall-to-wall. They finish one job on a Friday and are off on another job the following Monday. You do your file review and then the staff member responsible for the work on-site has to come back into the office. This may be a week or more after the review work has been completed, and then you require them to answer a page or more of queries on a job that is now somewhat hazy in the memory. The solution – whenever possible managers should seek to perform real time reviews – doing as much of the review work as possible while the job is in progress at the clients. Hopefully this real time reviewing will significantly reduce the number of outstanding review points remaining after the site work has been concluded. Alternatively, schedule time ahead for the staff member to come back into the office. Maybe they could also bring work back from the job they are now on so that time is not unaccounted for.

Make sure in the budget you have adequate time for the follow up of review points. To indicate what can go wrong I recall one job where the recovery rate on a £10,000 plus job was less than 50 per cent. This arose because the manager and partner decided between them to 'finish the job off' as the staff member responsible was out on another job.

It is also very easy to personalise problems – not just under recovery problems. It is always important to fix the processes and systems rather than the people. I recall hearing Horst Shultze speak on one occasion. Horst was the founder of the world famous Ritz Carlton hotel chain whose mantra was 'we are ladies and gentleman serving ladies and gentlemen'. He took personal responsibility for the three week training programme before the opening of each of the 60 plus Ritz Carlton hotels. His driving passion was to eliminate failures and errors. If there was a problem he ensured the staff were fully trained, equipped and empowered to eliminate the likelihood of the error reoccurring. Ritz Carlton is probably one of the more expensive hotel chains but their emphasis on quality guarantees their guests return.

> *"Mark, thank you for that very detailed and helpful response – My next point is that we do not advise clients regarding what we expect."*

Yes, this is a common problem. I think as an absolute minimum clients should receive a letter two months before the financial year end with an accompanying check list indicating what information you require for the purposes of completing your work. Then check a week or more before work is due to commence to ensure this is available and clarify anything regarding which the client is uncertain. Maybe last year's audit postscript records something that should be on this checklist? I know clients don't always play ball. But this is about having a good and proper process that manages as best you can what the client has to do for you given while they are your client, you are also their customer and they need to supply you with what you need so you can do your work efficiently.

> *"I am frustrated because staff do not keep the actual time analysis records up-to-date so I cannot tell where work has over run."*

Well, I have given you a few long answers so let's keep this one short. It is a general fact of life that staff tend to manage what is monitored. The culture as well as your required practice should compel, or maybe I should say propel everyone to follow company procedures. There are three points I would like to make. Firstly, up-to-date time analysis is the evidence staff are sensitive to the time constraints. Secondly, if work is performed outside the scope of the budget the question should be asked, *"should we raise this with our client?"* Finally, the accurate analysis of elapsed or consumed time is going to be the starting point for next year's budget – and remember the firm owner needs to be armed with the relevant information to discuss the question of fees and the scope of your work with the client.

> *"I appreciate the shorter response! So, next, I think we could identify additional services, but we don't have the time."*

Julian, this is a really important point. I understand when you know the job is going over budget looking around for other service opportunities is not necessarily high on your list of priorities. Yet, often managers know far more about the client's situation and needs rather than the partner. So, I recommend a two stage process. First, have everyone in the firm list out all the service solutions they believe they are able to provide. Accounts and audit staff will have a differing perspective on what they can offer when compared with firm owners. Next, fine tune the list and make sure, through an internal training session, you make staff aware of the need to be aware of cross serving opportunities and introduce staff to your *"Service Extension Opportunities"* form. Taking into account the opportunities identified, staff should list the services they see the client needs and an estimate of the fee or range of fees this service might generate. It is then the partner's responsibility to discuss this with the staff and then the client, and finally complete the *Service Extension Opportunities* as to whether the client is interested in any of these services. There you are, guess I'm back to my longer answers!

> *"Yes, well try this one now and, just a little bit shorter maybe Mark? Staff report back to me that they find some clients difficult to deal with."*

Yes, that is a difficult one to handle. It is a fact of life that not everyone welcomes the audit or accounting staff onto their premises. How to deal with this type of situation? Well it depends what the nature of the problem is but certainly staff must be forewarned regarding any likely personality challenges they might face and then the manager should be discreetly updated if work on site becomes too challenging. No one has the right to abuse another person and mutual respect is clearly of paramount importance. Your staff will, I trust, deal with these situations sensitively and ensure any inappropriate behaviour does not escalate. If problems persist then the firm owner really needs to talk with the staff and, if necessary, raise the matter with the client and ultimately even discuss with the client if they might be better served by seeking another firm.

> *"Mark – I now have my last manager problem which is that staff are not expected to feedback on job progress on a regular basis."*

OK, so let's give you the shortest answer of all! This is of course a two way responsibility – don't leave all the responsibility with the field staff. If you don't hear from the staff why not call or text them and ask, *"Is the job progressing according to plan? Are you having any unforeseen problems?"* The key all the time is having developed a realistic budget, is then to manage the staff and ensure the job is completed in line with budget.

WRITE DOWNS

This is a *really* important section.

There are two primary components of write downs or, as I shall also refer to them, variances. These two primary variances are 1) **sales** and 2) **productivity**.

Let me give an example. If a job is costed out, maybe by a manager, at £6,000 and the partner is, for whatever reason unable or unwilling to seek or gain the client's agreement to a fee of more than £5,000, then there is a sales variance of £1,000.

If this £6,000 job comes in at £7,000 then conversely there is a productivity variance of £1,000, in time costs greater than budgeted.

In working with managers of some mid-size firms I have learnt a great deal about productivity variances. My goal with managers is to coach and direct them toward achieving a minimum recovery of **95 per cent** of budget. One manager asked me why I did not require 100 per cent. It was a good question for which I did not have an immediate answer, except, I wished to appear reasonable in the hope my coaching would appear to be fair and my guidance would be accepted as being achievable. The firm was realising an average of 75 per cent overall of standard and so I was looking for some significant improvement.

The split between sales variance and productivity variance can be a hard one to identify on a firm-wide basis. Surveys with some firms I have worked with suggest **80 per cent** of the variances are productivity while as little as **20 per cent** are **sales** variances. One reason for this is that many managers seek to budget according to the expected fee which tends to the preparation of a budget that no one believes and no one follows. As a result the time elapsed to do the job is whatever it takes because the motivation to do the job based on the artificial and unrealistic budget does not exist. In reality I would expect the variances to be the other way round as it is essential to do all you can to minimise productivity variances so that you are left with mainly sales variances – which then gives the opportunity for some really good sales and negotiating training and development.

> **Key Point:** Allow managers to have the budget they have created and require them to keep to it.
>
> Work toward a target of at least 95 per cent of write downs being sales variances. Then have the partners attend a sales training program!

1 Follow this procedure:

- Build a 15 per cent pessimism quotient into all engagements
- The optimistic budget is only to control the job and motivate the engagement team
- Give the pessimistic budget to the client.

If the client's cutoff procedures for purchases, or despatch, or invoicing, or anything else have been poor for the last several years, what makes you think they are going to be any better this year? Yet you kid yourself and budget the job assuming everything will work well. We call this the optimistic budget. Optimistic budgets are okay for purposes of motivating the engagement team – giving them something to shoot for. The problem arises when you use the optimistic budget to estimate the price for the client.

Even if you analyse data objectively, you learn nothing unless the data is accurate. Unfortunately, some accountants go through a rigorous process of preparing a time budget, and then neglect to post the actual time spent on the various components. Thus, they cannot compare actual to budget. The time budget does little good unless you compare it with actual. Many accountants fail to keep systematic records to track results of their budget processes. The only number they know for sure is the total hours spent by each person. But that data is available from the time reporting system and does not enable the accountant to evaluate the performance of the ones who worked on the engagement. You should treat each line item on the time budget as a contract between the firm and the personnel who are to perform that part of the engagement. If they go over budget, you need to hold them accountable. But you have to know the actual time spent on each section.

2 Not specifying clearly what is included in the price estimate and what is not (then doing extras without charging for them)

Scope creep: A phenomenon where a project creeps beyond its original scope because the client keeps asking for additional services and the accountant provides them because there are no clear boundaries.

Yet accountants often do the same thing. They quote a client a monthly retainer or a fixed price for an audit or accounting engagement without specifying clearly what the engagement includes and – more important – does not include.

The key to avoiding this unpleasant situation is to hold two planning conferences:

- One with the client and
- One with the engagement team who will work the engagement.

> **Key point:** Scope creep can only occur with the willing consent of the accountant.

Scope creep doesn't 'just happen'. The accountant has to agree. Scope creep can come from the client's top management, but also from lower-level employees of the client who want some free help. Unfortunately, scope creep can also originate from an accounting firm employee who does 'favours' – extra free work for the client without consulting the partner.

There are two causes of scope creep: unclear project boundaries and a reluctance, unwillingness, or inability (you pick the word) within the accounting firm to stick to those boundaries.

Scope creep and small 'favours' are common in accounting practices.

3 Inefficiency (sometimes laid at the feet of the employee's supervisor)

Your firm time is an investment. When you or your employees work on a client's account you are investing your time. From this activity your clients require a return and so also does the firm. Consider this: every hour a person works has a cost to the firm. You might think of all working time (whether chargeable or non chargeable) as 'investment time'. Your people are either investing it on behalf of a client (chargeable time) or on behalf of the firm.

Here are a few ways to improve efficiency:

- Repeal Parkinson's Law. Employees spend so much time on engagements because of Parkinson's Law: "Work expands to fill the time available for its completion." If you give an employee an assignment without a time budget, they now have a new career. Give the employee a budget on every assignment – then hold them accountable.

- Work at the client's office. Working out of the office pays off for both owners and employees. You work more efficiently because you work straight through without interruption. If an employee needs information, he or she will find it easily from the client. In the office, the employee often leaves a message for the client and puts the file away to work on another engagement. This put away time and startup time drains efficiency.

- Exclude owner time from the budget.

- Post time backwards, with an 'hours remaining in budget'. This way the manager/senior sees a decreasing amount of time rather than an accumulating one.

- Post time daily. Have each person's time daily and compare it to budget. What gets monitored gets managed.

- Go to the client's to do your review.

- Make sure your employees have an extras work code. One reason you do not invoice such chargeable extras is that you do not find out about them because the employees have no place to post the time. Then, make sure you bill for the extras.

- Make sure employees remuneration is based partially on how well they meet budgets.

- Bad scheduling (whoever worked the job is either over- or under-qualified) or wall-to-wall scheduling.

- Bad supervision (*"Who? Me? No. But my other owners are the ones not performing!"*)

Too often accountants hide bad supervision by blaming their employees (*"That employee should have done that job in 12 hours."*) or bad scheduling (*"If I had the right person available for that assignment, we could have made budget."*) Those circumstances occur, but not as often as you pretend. When the job has gone over budget three years in a row, it is time to rethink your strategy.

Supervision is a complex issue involving, budgeting, and monitoring.

- Plan
- Budget
- Monitor

Inadequate skill in managing the client relationship; or lack of courage on the accountant's part (unwillingness to confront the client).

Important note: As explained earlier it is my firm belief that billing by the hour is no longer sustainable. Equally being paid in arrears is no longer a suitable practice. Virtually no one accepts payment in arrears other than monthly trade accounts.

QUESTIONS TO ASK YOURSELF

1
What is your gross margin?

2
What steps can you take to see this increase?

3
How will you monitor and armour this?

> A **GOOD PLAN** IS LIKE A **ROAD MAP**: IT SHOWS THE **FINAL DESTINATION** AND USUALLY THE **BEST** WAY TO GET **THERE**.
>
> H. STANELY JUDD

21 THE **COST** OF THE **EGO** TRIP

As a former accounting firm founder it was frustrating to learn that a well managed firm realises 85 per cent of standard time. Which surely means that by the time the job lands up for partner review and sign off the budget is all but fully expired. Not exactly the greatest of motivators to think that your [valuable] time is not going to be recovered.

If we assume that a job has been properly budgeted and that any client caused problems have either been within the boundaries of the unforeseen budget (usually about 5 per cent of the total budget) or the client has agreed to be billed for the extra work. Which of course is no more than the garage, builder, electrician or plumber would regard as normal and best business practice.

Often the higher level time (partner and manager) toward the back end of the job can run away with what little budget may remain. What do we call this time? It is *review* time. So, why call it the ego trip? Because to a large extent that is what I think it is...

COME WITH ME AND CONSIDER THIS SCENARIO...

The job has been finished and is now residing on the manager's desk. The manager is, of course, not going to review the job straight away and so staff move onto their next job – either in or maybe out of office.

Now, it is time for the manager to perform the review. This is, of course, where the manager displays his/her skills; their higher level of professional expertise. How does the manager proceed? The first page yields the first review point and this is reported as review note 1, *"You need to..."*, or *"Schedule 1 needs to..."*. Now the creative juices are flowing, the frustration of staff who should know better. Soon we are onto the second page and then the third. As the file review comes toward its climax the manager looks and sees that the fourth page is all but complete. *"Can I possibly make it onto a fifth page? They really should have done better than this!"*

Now, you may or may not recognise that scenario but trust me I know from the faces I see at seminars when I go into 'sketch mode' that this really happens. But wait I have not finished...

The staff are hauled off their current job and look aghast at the notes – *"How could there possibly be so many review points?"* the staff think. So, conscientiously the staff set to work on responding to the manager's review points. Sarcasm is off the agenda but if the staff person's brain could be hooked up to loudspeakers – there would need to be a censor on hand to bleep out all those dark inner thoughts.

Review points duly completed the file is returned to the manager who promises to clear the file very shortly.

The next week the staff find out there are just a couple more review points…

NOW IT IS TIME FOR THE PARTNER TO SHINE

Eventually, with pride and satisfaction the file is sent onward and upward to the partner's office. The partner smiles and mentions that the file had been expected and that it would be looked at shortly.

A few days later time is found to review the file. Now we are at the highest level of the firm where expertise is at its peak. As the partner opens the file and starts the review there is a real sense of excitement coupled with unbelief. *"How could this have been overlooked?"* the partner wonders.

Sometimes the review points reach to the foot of the page and on other occasions a second page is required. At the end the partner senses that the review points reflect superiority – the higher level of expertise that partners collect when entering the gates of partnerhood.

You think that is all far stretched? So none of that happens in your office? Well done. But if it does what is the effect, and more important, what is the remedy?

THE EGO IS ON DISPLAY

So managers display their superior expertise then this is followed by the partners. Each displaying their skills recorded for all to see. There is a lot of ego in this area and it is costing profitability.

THE EFFECT

Time and money. Probably a lot of it.

Time

How long does it take from the time that a job is finished to the time the job is completed (reviewed, completed and billed)? I may only have anecdotal evidence that this takes too long but I rarely see frowns when I mention this in my seminars. On the contrary, I usually see smiles. Smiles that tell me that some things don't change. Let's take an example of a job that from the time it is started to the time it is completed and billed takes 40 days. I often suggest that the first part of doing the job sometimes occupies about 20 per cent of the time (in this case 8 days of solid time on) while reviewing the job (manager and partner) and finally completing it can occupy as much of 80 per cent (in this case 32 days) of the time. Given that timeliness is key, time on job reviews is increasingly important and an area where job profitability can be improved.

I was once the manager of an audit team of 12 who were engaged in the audit of C&J Clark, the shoe footwear company. The staff were on site at Street, Somerset with me for three weeks and by the time they left I had not only reviewed all the audit work but also attended to all the partner review notes. As we left the job was complete - even the London based tax manager had been on site finalising the tax provisions.

Questions to consider:

- What is the average length of time (in days) from the time a job is finished to the time it is completed and billed for? Maybe select a cross selection of types of job.
- How many hours are charged to finish the job off?
- Calculate your finishing efficiency?

$$\frac{\text{Hours to complete}}{\text{Days x 7.5}} \times 100 = \text{Finishing efficiency}$$

* Insert your standard day in hours if different from 7.5

Money

While you could look at the cost of manager/partner review in total I think that for the purposes of establishing the cost of the ego trip it is important to look at the chargeable cost of the reviews that exceeds the budgeted cost of those reviews. Note partners should have a separate budget for review which is separate from meetings with the client to discuss the financial statement.

The file review by both managers and partners is an essential aspect of professional practice but the accumulation of review points is evidence of work perceived to be incomplete by staff in the pursuance of their duty. The raising of a review note takes time, answering it takes time and reviewing the action to clear takes time.

Can this review time be reduced? I believe it can and in so doing the overall length of time to complete will also be reduced.

How?

First of all it is important to establish your recurring review points (RRPs). You may need to review 10 to 15 files in order to establish a firm-wide account of RRPs. These should include both manager and partner RRPs.

A goal needs to be established to work toward eliminating these review points.

There are a number of steps to take – I will outline them here and that will enable you to determine your own preferred strategy.

Training

Hold a training session and discuss with the staff the RRPs so they know why each review point is raised and what they need to do to ensure that these RRPs do not appear in future reviews. This should include all manager RRPs and as many of the partner RRPs that staff can be held accountable for.

It is probably better not to cover more than 10 RRPs in any one session so select those that recur regularly.

Next this needs to be reinforced, here are some options:

- Include a RRP check list on each file
- Include your RRP checklist together with any additional commentary on your intranet.
- Have a designer create a poster of these RRPs. I have a client who has done this – the poster has been attractively designed and sits in the staff area. Personally I like this approach as it is creative and makes the point. While the first two work they are more traditional.

The key then is to hold each staff person accountable for ensuring they do not see these RRPs on any of their jobs.

Now onto partner RRPs. The first ask is for partners to move on from being nit pickers. Ouch! Nit picking review points should be included on the list for staff. So, let's avoid RRPs that are not really important. Now there are the important ones. Often managers have the same qualification as partners or, at least are qualified by experience. What are the partner RRPs? As with the staff managers need to take steps to eliminate partner RRPs.

BEFORE WE CONCLUDE...

We have thus far looked at improving job efficiency from the job review process.

There is one further ongoing recommendation which may help identify areas for internal training.

It is important to have staff feedback regarding areas they have identified on a job where their skills were not as complete or efficient as perhaps they should be. To address this I recommend that at the conclusion of each job they complete the following form, or better enter the information up on the firm's intranet. The form need only be simple – as an example:

TRAINING UPDATE

Staff :_____ Client: _____

As a result of completing the above job, these are the three main areas where I feel that further training would be helpful.

	AREA WHERE I NEED HELP	EFFECT ON THIS JOB	ACTIONED
1			
2			
3			

These feedback points could either be addressed with the staff member on an individual basis if the issue relates to just that one staff person. Alternatively, why not establish a monthly or quarterly training programme that includes addressing points raised on the Training Updates?

The results?

Hopefully these steps will reduce the managers and partners RRPs. In turn this should reduce the time taken to clear jobs and increase profitability.

The need for partners and managers to showcase their expertise is then more focussed on how we can better serve the client.

QUESTIONS TO ASK YOURSELF

1
How much do you estimate the ego trip costs you?

2
What are your RRPs?

3
Do you plan to introduce feedback on training needs?

> A **PLAN** IS A LIST OF **ACTIONS** ARRANGED IN **WHATEVER SEQUENCE** IS THOUGHT LIKELY TO **ACHIEVE** AN **OBJECTIVE**.
>
> JOHN ARGENTI

22 CORE SERVICES

WHAT ARE YOUR CORE SERVICES?

Here is a suggested list – you may have others but check to see if you can add any of these services:

> **Can do** - you have the expertise to deliver this type of work
>
> **Need to develop** - you need to develop the expertise
>
> **On my website** - this is showcased as a firm service
>
> **Paper marketing** - included in brochure cards etc
>
> **Reception** - details on our menu cards
>
> **Meetings** - to be discussed with clients in meetings

CORE SERVICES	CAN DO	NEED TO DEVELOP	ON MY WEBSITE	PAPER MARKETING	RECEPTION	MEETINGS
Accounting						
Advisory and planning						
Audit and assurance						
Accounting resources						
Bookkeeping						
Business advisory services						
Business valuations						

CORE SERVICES | 22

B-BBEE verification (SA only)						
B-BBEE consulting (SA only)						
Business rescue						
Cloud services						
Computer forensics						
Estate planning						
Forensic accounting						
Human resources						
Internal controls						
International tax						
Independent reviews						
Liquidations						
Litigation support						
Matrimonial reports						
Mergers and acquisitions						
Outsourcing						
Overhead cost reduction						
Profitability enhancement						

Payroll outsourcing					
Small business services					
Sourcing financing					
Tax compliance – corporate and individuals					
Tax consulting					
Trusts and estates					
Valuation services					
VAT services					
Wealth advisory					

QUESTIONS TO ASK YOURSELF

1
What does the full range of your core services look like?

2
How do you plan to inform staff and then require them to identify service opportunities?

3
How will you market these services? Service cards? Website?

> AS FOR THE **FUTURE**, YOUR **TASK** IS NOT TO **FORESEE** IT, BUT TO **ENABLE** IT.
>
> ANTOINE DE SAINT EXUPERY

23 SPECIALIST SERVICES

After your core service portfolio – how else can you expand your service offering so that you occupy more time and space in your clients' lives?

INDUSTRIES/SPECIALISATION

In order to promote a specific area of industry expertise it is key that you actually do have clients – preferably at least three or more in that sector. Clients will expect to be able to discuss industry relevant issues and consider that you do have expertise in their operational field. It is also important to have at least one member of staff who has expertise in that sector.

Here are some areas where you may have clients and could seek to involve a niche service offering:

INDUSTRIES/SPECIALISATION	CAN DO	NEED TO DEVELOP	ON MY WEBSITE	PAPER MARKETING	RECEPTION	MEETINGS
Agriculture						
Apparel						
Architects and engineers						
Art galleries and artists						
Asset backed lenders						
Bio science						
Broker dealers						
Car dealerships						
Charities						

Clean tech					
Colleges and universities					
Construction					
Consumer/retail					
Creative and digital					
Dealerships					
Debt restructuring					
Dentists and dental practices					
Diamond and jewellery					
Distribution					
Education services					
Emerging businesses					
Energy and renewables					
Engineering and design					
Entertainment and sports					
Family and closely held businesses					
Fashion					
Financial services					

Food – growers, distributors and grocers						
Gaming						
Government contractors						
Health care						
High tech						
High net worth individuals						
Hospitality travel and tourism						
Insolvency						
Insurance						
Investment companies						
I.T. and computer consultants						
Law firms						
Life science and technology						
Manufacturing and wholesale						
Media and entertainment						
Mining						

Modelling agencies					
Not for profits					
Nurseries					
Oil and gas					
Private equity groups					
Professional services					
Property based businesses					
Property management					
Real estate					
Shipping and logistics					
Small businesses					
Sports professionals and businesses					
Technology businesses					
Transportation					
Utilities					
Venture capitalists					

QUESTIONS TO ASK YOURSELF

1

What are your specialist services?

2

How can you increase your success with these services?

3

How can you increase your value/price?

> **IT IS NOT THE STRONGEST OF THE SPECIES THAT SURVIVE, NOT THE MOST INTELLIGENT, BUT THE ONE MOST RESPONSIVE TO CHANGE.**
>
> **CHARLES DARWIN**

24 PROFIT ENHANCEMENT STRATETIGIES

While most of the Double Your Income chapters address issues that focus on improving the results derived from an accounting practice I wish to ensure that we do not overlook looking more widely at the those aspects that relate to the management of any business.

From 1998 to 2002 I worked with Barry Schimel, Gary Kravtiz (USA) and Tim Levey (UK) in developing a series of tools designed to help accountants work with their client to improve the profitability of their business. Barry and Gary wrote a number of books including 100 Ways to Win the Profit Game while Tim wrote Profit Improvement in 7 steps. This chapter is based on what I learnt along my journey with these three profit improvement consultants. For a full understanding of profit improvement according to Messrs Schimel, Kravitz and Levey their books are highly recommended.

1 GUARDING AGAINST THEFT [OF TIME]

While theft may not be something you regard as an issue, the theft of time can be.

Recently, my wife visited our hairdresser (a former client of my practice and one with the reputation of being the best hair salon in Bristol). The owner was more than a little annoyed because the barber who does my hair had taken time off for his grandmother's funeral and advised her he was not planning to return until the New Year. As this was around Christmas he was fully booked and the salon owners were left cancelling some appointments and having to hire in another barber over this busy period. In another instance I have a client who has a number of problems with staff being off unwell on a regularly occurring basis and even staff who were supposed to be on courses who had decided to 'skip' the course.

One of the primary issues arising from this is that other staff know what is going on and are watching how you respond.

Do you hold a back to work interview when staff have been unwell for more than, say, two days? While you do not wish to encourage staff to return to work until fully recovered neither do you wish the sick leave to last longer than appropriate.

While on the subject of theft the same principle applies to the write up of time sheets. Staff should know that recording time accursedly is essential. Charging time that has not been spent is, potentially, unfair to the client whose costs sheets bears the unspent time. Not recording time, especially if it is out of normal hours time is unfair to staff – even though their motive well be not to be unfair to the client. Eventually this could become a habit with a number of possible knock-on effects.

Interestingly, it is often the firm owners who are in first and out last and yet have time sheets that only reflect a standard working week. This can establish an unhealthy culture of expectancy – a situation, which some people tell me, is a feature of some of the big accountancy firms they have worked for.

2   IDLE ASSETS

Do you have any assets lying around that are no longer being used? If so they are taking up space while they are gathering dust. Could you dispose of these either by donating them to charity or by selling on sites such as gum tree/eBay?

3   PAYMENT OF BILLS

Pay bills when they are due – but not before.

If, like many accountants you are incurring financing costs by borrowing working capital from a bank, it makes absolutely no sense to provide your creditors with interest-free use of your funds. Make sure your accounts payable staff do not pay bills any earlier than necessary.

Take advantage of purchase discounts.

4   CONTROL SERVICE CONTRACT EXPENSES

Almost whenever you purchase equipment the supplier tries to sell you a service contract. Most companies buy into it. But it's expensive and not always necessary. Perform an audit of your existing service contracts. Are you paying for any for which you no longer use the equipment? Would a regular maintenance schedule for your equipment minimise the need for that service contract? Better still, is there anyone on your staff who could repair it more effectively and quickly?

5   DEVELOP FINANCIAL "FLASH REPORTS"

Remember the maxim that informs us that you manage what you monitor? Many businesses will thrive if management obtains early warning signals of financial opportunities. Could you develop a flash report that perhaps tracks recovery rates, time on performances, billings? Identify the areas that are of significance to the firm and start producing flash reports. Consider how these can be integrated onto the partner's dashboard.

6 DASHBOARDS

Following on from flash reports, do you have a practice management system that includes a dashboard? If not then is there one available in your marketplace?

Software system suppliers have realised that the dashboard is an important component of practice management.

Dashboards can provide instant answers to:

- Which are our most/least profitable clients?
- Who are our most/ least productive staff?
- What's the current turnaround time on jobs?
- What profit are we making out of a job?
- How effective are our credit control processes?
- What's our exposure to risk?
- What progress are we making with our current workload and what's still outstanding?
- How are we spending our time and how much of it is chargeable?

Features can include:

- Improved management control via at-a-glance views of your business performance
- Set up and monitor, through a single dashboard, the key performance indicators that matter most to your business, such as:
    - Income growth (%) for the business and by partner
    - Debtor days
    - Lockup value and days
    - Percentage of chargeable/non-chargeable time
    - Partner and business profitability per client
    - Staff performance and profitability

7   OUTSOURCING

In the late 1990s the UK saw a number of Indian companies seeking to promote outsourcing to India where labour costs are much lower. But are standards lower? Over the past forty or more years citizens of India have trained as Chartered/Chartered Certified Accountants and the staff who work in these companies are often CAs/CPAs.

I recently met a practitioner at his home office in Oxford who introduced me to his four staff. Except the images of his staff were all projected onto his lounge wall as they were all based in India. That, at least brought home to me the reality of the power of outsourcing.

I know firms in both the UK and US who have successfully outsourced all their Tax Returns to an Indian accounting and tax agency.

Flipping the coin, some of the larger London-based accounting firms have moved some of their [tax] departments to other parts of the UK where staff costs are not as great as in the City of London.

With a further flip – if you 'enjoy' low labour costs and have a high level of IT infrastructure could you offer outsourced services to other accountancy firms?

8   FORM YOUR OWN TEAM INTO OF PROFIT ADVISORS

While managing my publishing company I developed a strategic relationship with a Chicago based organisation that was also delivering marketing solutions to accountants. One of their most successful newsletters was the Profit Improver which was conjoined to a programme that was associated with training enabling accountants to deliver profit improvement services to their clients. As this organisation's sales were escalating and their member conferences packed to the rafters I decided to negotiate the UK rights to the Profit Improvement system. I then contracted with Reeves & Neylan, a UK accounting firm based in London and the south east to use this american material to develop something that would work in the UK.

This enabled us to sell and train UK accountants a service that encouraged them to advise clients to help them increase their profitability. It also provided them with a valuable USP.

Profitability might not be the primary purpose of the business but is certainly one of the key outcomes that is essential for owners. Without it there is no purpose in the owner continuing to engage their skills in the development of the enterprise.

WHAT DID WE LEARN?

One of the lessons we all learnt is that improving profitability is the responsibility of everyone in the organisation not just the firm leaders.

We learnt that the profit and loss account had a limited role to play in helping business leaders identify where profits could be increased.

We were reminded of the old adage that tells us that sales is vanity, profit is sanity and cash is reality.

Along the way we learnt to teach our members how to play the 'profit game' with clients.

THE PROFIT GAME

I first saw this 'game' played when I attended a member firm training session with a CPA firm in Detroit and was amazed how much 'unrealised firm profit' those participating were able to identify.

Let me at this point establish that this is not a game as we know it but a really insightful team process that brings team spirit and ingenuity to the fore.

It's a game that seeks to identify what are called 'profit robbers.' That is those costs or activities that serve to restrict or reduce the profits of the enterprise.

So, imagine you are in a room with your team – not just owners or directors. Depending on how many there are in your organisation this easily works well with up to about 12 people.

Introduce the team members to the concept of profit robbers and help them understand how to recognise a profit robber.

Profit robbers are recognised by three prefixes. [I still think that the flip chart remains one of the best available management tools.] So complete with flip chart ask your team, *"What costs or activities do you know that are causing us to lose profits that begin with... 'Mis.'"*

You might start by marking on the flip chart such words as 'mistake,' 'misunderstand' but soon all the team will be on board with this innovative approach to team management. But this is more than a game as you are not only seeking to find the profit robbers but to arrest them!

Other words you might hear? There are too many to list and besides giving you too many answers might just take the fun out of the game. These words should describe what is going on in your company that should not be. Some examples include:

> Mismanage
>
> Misplace
>
> Mistake
>
> Misunderstand

Misprice

Misuse

Misrepresent

Missed deadlines

When you sense the energy waning and having filled up your flip chart it is time to introduce your next profit robber. Words that begin with... 'Re.'

Redo

Reanalyse

Return

Rethink

Remake

Revise

Restock

Retrain

Redo

Redeliver

Reposition

Now you are in the full flow of tapping into your team's sense of fun and knowledge of what is going on in their neck of the woods. One more profit robber and then let the real work begin!

Our final profit robbers are found when we look at words that begin with... 'Un.'

Unbilled

Unclear

Undone

Unnecessary

Unfocused

Unrealistic

Underperforming

Unprepared

Unused

So now you have a whole list of profit robbers on three or maybe more flip chart pages all generated by your team. And note, none of these profit robbers appear anywhere in the profit and loss account, unless repairs has crept in!

Depending on how many you have participating in the game you can either split the group into three or maybe have them work together over a series of three meetings. Now is the time to drill down further into what exactly does each word.

> **Ask:**
>
> How does [insert your first profit robber] cause us to lose profitability?
>
> What do we [all] need to do to catch and eliminate this drag on our profits?

RESULTS

The profit robber game works. I have known organisations that have identified over £1 million in unrealised profit, or up to 50 per cent increase in profits. You must be constantly vigilant in identifying activities that rob your bottom line of its profit potential and do all you can firm-wide to minimise them, if not eliminate them altogether.

Every profit robber you arrest will create more bottom line opportunities for you. The additional profits realised will add value to your business and create competitive advantages. They will enable you to capitalise on financial opportunities that were previously unattainable.

Looking for further ideas? Barry Schimel led the first ever profit improvement session I attended in Detroit. See if you can find one of his books out on the internet. One book to look out for is *100 ways to win the profit game.*

Why not try this with your own team and find your own profit robbers. And then maybe with your clients?

Mis..

....

....

Re ....

....

....

Un..

....

....

9 PROTECT YOUR COMPANY'S MOST VALUABLE ASSET: YOURSELF

Don't let the strain of business put you out of commission. You are the most valuable business asset. I regularly come across firm owners who are showing symptoms of stress. The causes cited include too much work pressure, staff problems, financial problems, domestic challenges – and, to repeat the one I hear the most – too much work pressure.

In the final analysis, your health and well-being are your responsibility. Resist the urge to work yourself into a sick bed. We all live our lives in accordance with our priorities. Balance in all things is essential.

Clearly I have no expertise in the area of health, but allow me to at least pass on a few of the strategies I have employed to keep stress under control. But not before I share that I have been a person that some would describe as a workaholic – not that I would agree with that analysis of course! I have also had my fair share of times when I would admit to worry, anxiety, work pressure, financial challenges and so on. But stress? No, never. So first lesson – don't be in denial but use the word stress or stressed out sparingly.

Cause: If I restrict this to work causes, which I will, then I have probably one of the main verbalised causes of stress – too much work. But is that really the case? Look at stress as a result or 'fruit' of decisions or situations and then dig deep to identify the causes.

Some of those causes are in your control – others are not. For example, if you are a two-owner firm and your fellow partner suffers a serious accident or is diagnosed with a life threatening illness these are events that are likely to add to your workload – with limited notice but significant impact.

Alternatively, imagine you are 60 or thereabouts and have managed your finances carefully. Retirement is around the corner and then the stock market crashes and your asset/income spread sheet now tells a somewhat differing story of the [financial] future.

WORK PRESSURE. WORRY. ANXIETY. STRESS?

While I admit to having declared that I was, on occasions, stressed my normal default is to see myself as being anxious – and at times, overly anxious.

The reality, as I see it, is that if you look at the causes of stress we come to realise that they are often self-inflicted. The good news is that if you identify and address these areas in your own life/business then the occurrences of anxiety/stress may well reduce - or even evaporate altogether!

Allow me to suggest a few (I am sidestepping the domestic ones] that I come across - and a brief remedy. And before you read the remedy, you will already know the solution to your own situation and that may differ from mine.

NO	CAUSE	REMEDY SUGGESTION
1	Too much work	Cancel out those lower end clients that are the cause of some of that stress. Delegate more of your work. Train staff in areas where further expertise/knowledge is required. Set a minimum fee policy and avoid taking on lower end business. Stop allowing work to butt up against deadlines
2	Too much month and not enough money	This has been a long-standing problem in the accountancy profession. Remedy is simple – but I am not saying it is simple to implement. Those things that are really worth doing rarely are. Have clients pay you by direct debit – in their accounting year.
3	Staff issues	It depends what they are of course. But, your success here is going to be observed by everyone else in the firm. Succeed in this area and you will influence others to step up to the mark – or else. Your ultimate sanction is cancelling staff out. I know firms who have cancelled non-performing partners so why not staff. Attributes? Determination to come out a winner while ensuring that there are no losers.
4	Client issues – out of your depth	Recognise your capability and seek good counsel. Invest in developing your own expertise. Pass the client onto others – even if they are outside of your firm.

PROFIT ENHANCEMENT STRATEGIES | 24

| 5 | Client issues – made a mistake? | Own up as soon as possible – don't cover up. Share with someone else in your firm – a problem shared is a problem halved. Remember you have insurance so do you need to contact your professional indemnity insurers? What lessons are there to be learned so that the situation does not reoccur? |
| 6 | Work-life balance out of kilter | Do all you can to stop this being a perpetual problem. This is not fair to you, your staff or your loved ones. Do what it takes to stop working beyond that which is fair and reasonable You decide but keep it to less than 50 hours a week – please). There are 8760 hours in a year, 8784 in a leap year – make sure not all your life is spent focussed on work. When at home – be at home. |

QUESTIONS TO ASK YOURSELF

1

Have you thought of playing the Profit Game and looking for those profit robbers?

2

What do you need to do to protect yourself?

3

Do you plan to develop a cost minimisation plan?

> FOR **WHAT** WILL IT **PROFIT** THEM TO **GAIN** THE WHOLE **WORLD** AND **FORFEIT** THEIR **LIFE**?
>
> **JESUS AS RECORDED IN MARK 8:36**

25 MARKETING

> **My definition of marketing**
>
> Marketing comprises all those activities that enable you to identify opportunities to advance your pursuit of winning new business.

In the thirty years I have been privileged to serve accountants there has been one constant with regard to feedback concerning winning new clients and that is that most new business comes from existing client referrals. Surveys show for many firms this as much as 90% of their new business.

Thus, this book has endeavoured to highlight ways in which you can assess your own performance in a range of areas. We started our time together by looking at the LUBRM and TUBR models identifying the keys to an accounting firm's profitability.

Clients are unlikely to recommend you if they are not satisfied with your service or do not consider them to be value for money. Clients tend to view every bill on the basis of the value they have received. If they believe you and your firm represent good value they will recommend you. People also do business with people – not just you, but your staff – everyone in the organisation will leave an impression on clients. A positive impression and they will be happy to recommend, but if clients aren't happy with the interaction with the team at your firm, they might not leave, but they may not think of recommending you either. If you scored well on the scorecard you have the ingredients for your clients (assuming you ask them) to be willing to recommend your services.

HOW MUCH SHOULD YOU INVEST?

Rather than use the word 'spend' I always refer to marketing spend as an 'investment'. That is, in my mind, to upgrade it to a higher level than costs incurred in doing business today. Marketing is all about winning tomorrow's business. You incur a spend from which you need a return. That return may be defined as winning new clients or gaining new engagements from existing clients

Consultants typically recommend a spend of three per cent. But, inter firm surveys usually reveal a spend in the region of two per cent. However, it is not always easy to identify the actual spend as this is often spread over a range of profit and loss accounts such as printing and postage, advertising, website, entertaining and so on.

Global accounting firms spend is usually in the region of seven per cent.

Just as important as the cash you invest is the time committed to firm development by partners. I strongly recommend a lower benchmark - an absolute minimum of 200 hours per annum.

EXTENSION SERVICES AND CROSS-SERVING CLIENTS

Your existing clients are also candidates for your extension services. Can you identify five services that you can deliver that your clients need? It could be bookkeeping; VAT, PAYE, IT, management accounts, management meetings, estate planning, IHT planning, financial planning and so on. Have each firm owner list their top 20 clients and then across the top of the table list these five extension services. You will now have 100 service opportunities. Some will not be applicable to a particular client, others, may already have been delivered. That said, this list of services are ones that need constant delivery or revisiting.

	SERVICE EXTENSIONS – CROSS SERVING OUR CLIENTS					
No.	Client	1	2	3	4	5
1	ABC	D				X
2	DEF			D	D	
3	GHI	X				
4	NJK	D	i	i		X
5	MNH				D	
6	MBG			D		
7	LKI			X		
8	LPI	D				D
9	DER					
10	VGY		D	i		
11	HGF		X	D		D
12	YYT					
13	KJH	X		X		X

14	OIU	i		X		
15	BNM		D			D
16	YTR	X				v
17	RFB			X	X	
18	MFW				i	
19	VGH		D	X		
20	BHJ					

Key

1-5: Your extension services   D: Service already delivered

i: Service introduced   X: Service not appropriate

Note: the blanks represent service opportunities – over a two to three year time period seek opportunity to see which of your clients are interested in these service extensions

While there is no doubt business to be retained, referrals from clients and extension services there are also new clients to be won through marketing.

There are many books that have been written on the subject of marketing as well as many seminars. My approach in this last chapter is to provide some good solid theory and then to suggest a series of marketing strategies and tactics to blend into your firm's marketing programme.

Marketing is not an activity that can be isolated or independent of other practice drivers. Marketing should be developed in context of the firm, its objectives, the objectives of the owners and the needs of clients. Thus the role of marketing must be integral to the firm's strategic planning.

If the firm is 'small' and intending to remain so then the required results from marketing will be determined by the owner(s). With an ever-increasing regulatory regime that involves deadlines, fines and penalties a sole practitioner, or even two-three partner firm may not wish to increase in size. Gross fees may increase steadily with clients lost by attrition replaced through referrals from clients and professional referrals. Ownership may not wish to grow at more than, say three to five per cent a year. More specifically ownership may not wish to grow the firm's total hours output.

Does marketing have a role to play in this situation? Yes, but the marketing activities will be influenced by ownership's agenda.

CROSS SERVING CLIENTS

My long standing friend and consulting colleague (US based) August Aquila wrote:

"There is a perennial problem in the accounting profession. Partners do not cross sell and hence are leaving countless dollars on the table, not providing clients with the best services and are risking client relationships.

The number one reason clients leave their current service provider is *"lack of service."* That's not too hard to understand. Clients have an issue at hand, they need help and they will find a service provider to help them.

None of us is good or great at doing everything. That's why we have partners.

So, why don't we use them?

Over the years, I have accumulated a list of reasons why partners don't cross sell. I'm sure that you can add your own. Here's my top ten:

10. Our compensation system does not reward us for cross selling or assisting in a cross selling activity
9. Partners in the firm do not have any specific goals. So, we just do what we think is best for the firm.
8. I won't get to bill the client for the work done by another partner.
7. Other partners won't understand the special needs of my clients.
6. Our firm (i.e., the management) does not require us to cross sell.
5. We don't track this or we don't have a firm-wide approach.
4. Why should I have someone else talk with my clients? What if they mess us?
3. What if the other partner makes me look bad in the eyes of the client?
2. Where am I going to find the time? I am already pretty busy.
1. I really don't trust my partners to deliver."

MARKETING PLANNING

As night follows day a firm that delivers outstanding client service will have a good reputation among clients that will lead:

- to an increase in referrals, that will lead
- to an increase in new clients, that will lead
- to an enhanced reputation in the community

How can a firm grow and win business beyond those afforded by client referrals?

PLANNING TO GAIN NEW CLIENTS

Some firms manage themselves without any formal planning process. That's not to say there are no plans it's just that these are not formalised, so they may reside in the mind of one or more individuals, and others will generally be in the dark. In this situation, firm members' role is to work without a clearly defined understanding of the firm's plans. They may hear snippets of information, they may make certain assumptions and draw certain conclusions, but the big picture and how they fit into it is not necessarily clear. They may 'hear' about the plans, but they are not sure if or when these plans will come to pass.

The plan should be communicated to everyone in the firm and made available on the firm's network, possibly in an 'executive summary' format.

The advantage of this strategy is that in order to develop the plan, management must commit to the planning process, consider the firm's mission and take a look at how the future might transpire and what has to be done to enable the firm and its staff to realise their full potential in seeking to meet the needs of their clients.

Thus, what we have described in Double Your Income so far, we regard as the bare necessities for a successful an accounting practice. Alternatively, you could view our journey thus far as insights into best practice upon which you have your own views and you will with each of the activities we describe either agree or agree to disagree and be able to decide the extent to which you could improve in each of these areas.

Become convinced and captivated by planning and you will become an advocate for planning, not only for yourself and your firm **but also with clients,** which does of course provide a service delivery opportunity that you can personally vouch for as a necessity. You owe it to yourself, your co-owners and team members to be the best you can be. You owe it to clients to be the best accountant/adviser knowing that the community needs the value you bring to the marketplace. Put more succinctly, if you do not meet and exceed the expectations of the clients – someone else might take your place.

STEPS IN THE MARKETING PLANNING PROCESS

Firm owners need to take a wider look at the firm's business plan as this will provide the strategies to be addressed in the firm's strategic marketing plan. The firm's business plan impacts the development of the strategic marketing plan in areas such as desired growth and service development.

What is strategic marketing planning?

You need a clear understanding of who you are and what the firm is capable of, what business you are in, the value you create for your clients, and how you differentiate yourselves in winning and retaining clients. The key is to create the means to make the most of whatever your business environment presents. The task for owners is to create strategic thinking and develop strategic plans to create success.

Leadership is important

In the process of developing a plan, answers come through a careful process of creative thinking and logical reasoning that must be unique to your firm. The process of strategic planning or goal setting has fundamental features that make it relevant to almost any challenge facing any accounting firm. But leadership is vital to achieve success. Someone needs to put the right people in the right places and build a 'marketing culture' and a marketing team. Someone has to build consensus about the plan, communicate it widely and reinforce it frequently, and at least one individual needs to face difficult issues and make tough decisions.

Designing a strategy – how not to do it

There are those accounting firms that have a planning system that is bottom heavy. They spend a great deal of time getting all of those involved in client service, departmental and individual tactical plans in place, but little or no time thinking about the basic strategy or direction of the business. To correct this approach, some firms try to set firmwide goals, which can include tactics that involve the whole firm, such as starting a client satisfaction survey, or starting a marketing training programme for staff, or sending out regular press releases. These are examples of marketing tactics. Firms must go through the planning process before they begin doing these. Some firms create grandiose strategic plans, supported by elaborate detailed budgets, resource estimates, tactical plans and timetables, most of which ultimately have little connectivity to the success of the business.

Designing a strategy – how to do it

Think about the future. What services do your clients need? Where does your firm want to be in the next three to five years? Focus on 'futuring' as an integral element of your planning. Futuring should be used to form a picture of the direction in which you need to head. Be prepared to ask the tough questions such as: Is our tax return service becoming obsolete? Should we still focus on processing of tax returns? What will our staff do between 1 December (will this eventually be 1 October?) and 5 April? Should we use paraprofessionals? Should we hire staff on tax season contracts? Should we train our staff to focus on other growing/emerging areas of practice such as business valuations; technology consulting; HR consulting; estate planning; retirement planning and so on. While developing a plan is necessary, it should focus on the 'future' picture and how that picture will be drawn and completed?

Personal marketing plans (PMP)

Every firm owner and possibly the managers should have a PMP. On the basis that (some) managers aspire to firm ownership they should be involved with marketing as the ability to win new business should be one of the conditions for future participation in firm ownership.

The PMP is valuable for four reasons:

1. It helps the individual articulate their goals and become committed to their role in marketing
2. It helps you manage your referral programme so that firm owners have firm-strategic relationships
3. It provides you with a way to assign marketing budgets to individuals
4. Everyone who has a PMP will have prospects.

In order to prepare your own PMP it is important to look carefully at a number of areas. I have identified some of these in the following survey.

How you use this information will depend on how structured your firm's approach is to marketing, who is responsible and what marketing's requirement is of individual firm owners. You may have a separate marketing function or marketing may be wholly the domain of the firm owners. You may have a telemarketing team and a sales team but the reality is that you need to fulfil your responsibility to broadcast the firm's service capability and gain new business.

It is a fact of life that you will lose some clients. Organic growth may or may not replace business lost through attrition. Gaining clients cannot be the sole or even primary responsibility of your clients acting as your advocate.

You may not have a marketing qualification but you do have a marketing responsibility. Marketing provides a wonderful opportunity to present your service capabilities. It does however require you to accept that you will not always succeed.

Let's have a closer look at you, your clients and set the scene for preparing your own PMP with the following survey.

PERSONAL MARKETING SURVEY

This survey is to assist you in the formulation of your role in marketing firm services. This form may be downloaded from marklloydbottom.com - downloads.

1. How would you describe your next likely good client? This may take into account turnover, profitability, size of organisation or any other parameters you may consider appropriate.

2. List your main active professional referral sources and the approximate number of leads they have referred to you in the last 12 months.

	NAME	PROFESSION	ORGANISATION	NO. OF LEADS
1				
2				
3				
4				
5				
6				
7				
8				
9				
10				

3. What marketing activities work for you?

Using the scale below, rate the effectiveness in your opinion of the following marketing activities for winning new clients.

4 = Excellent   3 = Good   2 = Fair   1 = Poor

Professional referrals ....

Client referrals ....

Social media ....

Firm website, Apps, newswires ....

Other (please list):

....

....

....

....

4. In which areas would you like to extend or improve your marketing?

5. How long do you spend marketing the firm's capabilities?

6. What do you find are the benefits of the firm's existing marketing activities?

7. What are your areas of:

TECHNICAL EXPERTISE

1. ....

2. ....

3. ....

INDUSTRY SPECIALISATION

1. ....

2. ....

3. ....

8. What are your top three strengths:

1. ....

2. ....

3. ....

9. Please consider and record the value of new business you realistically expect to secure in the next 12 months:

New business I expect to secure: [£] _____

Or range: minimum [£] _____ to a maximum of [£] _____

10. Please estimate the potential for delivering additional services to your existing client base:

Minimum _____ Maximum_____ Realistic _____

11. Regarding your own marketing efforts:

What is succeeding?

What is not succeeding? Why not?

What would you like to improve or invest more time doing?

12. Which prospective clients are you currently targeting, current status and likely fees.

	PROSPECT	CURRENT STATUS ON A SCALE OF 1 TO 10 (10 - THEY ARE JUST ABOUT TO BECOME A CLIENT)	APPROX. FEE INCOME
1			
2			
3			
4			
5			
6			
7			
8			
9			
10			

13. List your top 15 clients. These may be identified by turnover, annual fee or size of client. This will provide you with the first attempt to specify those clients that are high on your list of prospects for a higher level of service

	CLIENT	TURNOVER/SIZE	FEE
1			
2			
3			
4			

5			
6			
7			
8			
9			
10			
11			
12			
13			
14			
15			

14. Please make any further notes that you consider important at this time to the development of your marketing activity.

15. Identify the top 5 strengths and weaknesses of the firm.

These are internal to the firm.

STRENGTHS

1. ....
2. ....
3. ....
4. ....
5. ....

WEAKNESSES

1. ....
2. ....
3. ....
4. ....
5. ....

16. Please note your club memberships and any position held:

MEMBERSHIP	POSITION HELD

17. Please rate, using the scale below, the following extension services.

5 = a must for all my clients

4 = an essential service for many of my clients

3 = a service I can see myself selling at least 6 times in the next year

2 = a service I can see myself selling between 1 and 6 times in the next year

1 = I can't see myself selling this service

	SERVICE RATING
BUSINESS MANAGEMENT	
Advice on bookkeeping and accounting systems	
Profit and cash flow forecasts	
Guidance on business structure	
Advice on remuneration packages	
Retirement and pension advice	
Consultancy – financial and management	
Profitability planning	
Other (please state):	
Other (please state):	

BUSINESS DEVELOPMENT	
Business acquisition advice	
Developing growth plans and strategies	
Other:	
Other:	
TAX PLANNING	
Minimising personal tax	
Minimising corporate tax	
Minimising inheritance tax	
Minimising capital gains tax	
Minimising national insurance	
PAYE/NIC health check	
VAT health check	
Other	
Other:	
ACCOUNTS	
Preparing management accounts	
Other:	
Other:	
PERSONAL	
Planning investment strategies	
Advising on trusts and covenants	
Advising on wills and executorships	
Other	
Other	

FUNDING	
Arranging or negotiating banking facilities	
Advice on loans, mortgages or other business finance sources	
Advice on loans	
Other	
Other	
INFORMATION TECHNOLOGY	
Computerisation	
Guidance on hardware systems	
Guidance on software systems	
Assistance in operator training	
Other	
Other	

PERSONAL MARKETING PLAN (PMP)

You should now be in a good position to prepare your own PMP. I have chosen not to include a template of a PMP because my experience of working with a standard template is that it does not work. At least mine do not seem to have done! I have also networked with marketing directors of accounting firms and they generally agree that accountants don't make good customers for boiler plate templates. So, that's good news that you are not required to conform!

But, I strongly recommend you decide what you are going to do with your marketing activities. You need to commit what you are going to do and I recommend printing this out and keeping it handy so that it doesn't get buried in whatever technology you are currently using.

QUESTIONS TO ASK YOURSELF

1

Do you have a marketing plan that is working?
If not, how will you improve it?

2

How much will you invest in marketing. Finance? Time?

3

What are your targets for new clients and
new engagements from current clients?

> HOW MUCH **TRAFFIC** TO YOUR **WEBPAGE** WILL YOU **LOSE** IF IT TAKES **LONGER** THAN **3 SECONDS** TO RELOAD. **40%**
>
> RAISSA EVANS, RUNNING RELOAD LLC

26 | FINAL GUIDANCE AND MAKING IT HAPPEN

And now to the path that leads to doubling your income:

- You might not have previously studied the art and science of practice management
- You might have attended management courses but not implemented as you intended
- You may not have a business degree
- You might have been sceptical about the potential for doubling your income especially if you are in a country with a low rate of inflation and threats to your compliance revenues

But, you are in business and every good business owner deserves to make a healthy profit.

HOW PROFITABLE IS YOUR BUSINESS?

What is the firm's profit *before* owner salary and profit share?

Then:

Deduct a market salary (a number that, I suggest, should not be less than six times the average wage for your country).

Then:

Deduct an amount that represents the return on owner capital employed in the business.

What is the result? This represents the true commercial profitability of the business? Many find that after making these adjustments the profit from the business is either non-existent or alarmingly low. Some, I know have even been trading at a loss.

Then look at your accessible personal income from the business. How much do you have to leave in to fund working capital? So, you could look at profit at the basic level as to what you actually have available to draw from the business.

RETIREMENT ON THE HORIZON

Are you under investing in your retirement funding? Have you made a commitment to invest more but been unable to do so? You will know what you should be investing – but are you able to prioritise salting the necessary funds away for the future? One statistic from a UK insurance company suggests that income requirement in retirement approximates to 65-70 per cent of pre retirement income. If you continue investing what you are today will your capital be sufficient to deliver your required income? Given fluctuations and stock markets and interest rates – what margin do you have? If the answer is 'not enough' then increasing your income for this purpose alone should be a powerful driver. Your income today has to achieve these two primary goals:

1. Provide sufficient income for today to enable you to live as you determine, and
2. Provide the funds for investment so that you can live comfortably in retirement

I once consulted with Jerry Atkinson of Atkinsons, Albuquerque, NM, USA. During my time with Jerry he shared this insight, *"Mark, I have always employed the very best – not the cheapest."* He then went onto say that he intended to have his 'go to hell money' by the time he was 55. As I have strong Christian beliefs I was arrested by his terminology – which I did not quite follow. *"What is your go to hell money Jerry?"* I asked. *"I plan to be financially independent by the time I am 55 so that if I need to I can tell my partners to go to h____ "* he replied.

At the time I was enjoying significant growth in my practice and this included generating significant financial services commission.

I was 39 and returned back to my accountancy practice determined to become financially independent by 55. Based on this conversation I developed a key proposition that I employed when discussing retirement planning with clients and the importance of being financially intentional regarding the necessity to invest for later life. For many years I used this one liner to remind myself about saving for the future while provoking clients to be realistic about the ability of the final sale of the business to raise sufficient funds for retirement.

> *"A good business person should be capable of being financially independent by the time they are 55."*

Some people say they do not plan to retire because they enjoy work so much. For others, retirement is far off and not high on today's agenda. But, as the Romans taught us, 'tempus fugit.' Time flies so don't delay reviewing your plans and upgrading investment levels if appropriate. Better to create margin today because we do not know what tomorrow will bring. We should be cautious about how much we presume on the future – none of us can be certain about what our future health or life's goals will look like.

These are aspects of life and thinking that have motivated me in the past – but what about you?

PROFIT SHARING

This is a big subject but one that does have a major impact on profitability. We looked earlier at the LUBRM model and the bottom line which was expressed as Net Income Per Partner. You will never maximise profitability if you split the bottom line equally. Look back at benchmark 23 in chapter 3 for evidence of the way firms creatively profit share.

The fault line in sharing profits equally is that it generates no real momentum or motivation for partners to improve their performance. Further, not all partners are equal in their contribution to firm results. The lock step system enables [older] owners to continue to receive a large share of the profits while younger partners await their turn for a greater share. But maybe that model is perhaps broken and causing concern among some younger partners? In any event it is partly responsible for profit stagnation.

The underlying objective of not splitting equally is to motivate everyone to stretch and achieve outstanding results that will result in the firms' profits increasing so that everyone gains. The fact that one partner receives more than another should be a reason to congratulate recipients not one to begrudge the financial success of others.

How might benchmarking help us better understand good profit share principles?

1. Often the partner with the highest income may be receiving 1.5 - 3.0 more than the partner with the lowest income. That is smaller firms at the lower end and larger firms at the upper

2. Newly admitted equity partners will typically on average receive about two thirds the average income of all partners

3. How are managing partners remunerated compared to the partner group? The firm leader has historically received greater profit share than the rest of the partners. It was expected as a reward for reaching the top job, and for assuming the responsibilities the role comes with. However, times have changed and now in firms participating in the IPA survey this is only the case with about 40 per cent of firms. The highest paid partners are often those who win the firm a lot of new business year on year.

The three components of sharing the profit pie are:

1 Salary

It is important to provide all firm owners with a basic salary. Again, not all partners are equal so how to determine salary levels? For smaller firms (maybe less than 6 or 7 owners) a straw poll system could be employed. That has the advantage of giving all partners input and making a fair judgment on one another. If there are more than this number it is not necessarily easy for one person to assess the value and contribution of another so the salary will likely be determined by either a remuneration committee or the managing partner. There are other options but these are the common methods.

2 Equity

There is always room for a tranche of profits to be split based on seniority and firm equity.

3 Profit Sharing

The first two profit allocations may well account for up to 70-75 per cent of the profit share leaving 25-30 per cent for distribution based on performance in the areas the partner group determine are important to enhance performance and profitability.

> **Key Point:** Consultants to the accounting profession overwhelmingly agree that a firm will never maximise profitability if profits are either split equally (or there is a preponderance of equal sharing) or based on seniority.

OVERCOMING THE TWO MAIN OBJECTIONS

There are usually two main objections:

1. Those who refuse to consider change because there is a partnership agreement that has worked and *"there is no need to change what has worked in the past."* Which of course really means, *"I am concerned my income will reduce."*

Observations and overcoming

This is a common objection. To overcome this there needs to be a change of mind-set and that may occur if partners agree that an individual's profit share in the future will not be less than would have been received under the old system.

2. Envy. Oh yes. Envy that one [maybe younger partner or a rainmaker] might make more than some of the others. I hope they do – that way as the firm grows the profits from the young talent and new business will keep on growing.

Observations and overcoming

Move on please. It is to everyone's advantage to unleash the power of your team's talent. Reward and motivate them, as profit share is a real issue for many who have debt and aspirations. Celebrate with them when they do well – and encourage them to do even better next year.

I think it is an advantage to require the owner team to achieve greatness. I have seen far too often owners who have had their rewards almost compounded or annuitised through systems such as the points based approach. I have also seen partners whose performance has not just plateaued but gone into steep decline.

My own view, and it is a personal one is that when the age of 55 is reached the profit share should level out – maybe even decline to allow the younger [performing] partners to participate.

AVOIDING FTI

Procrastination is an enemy of implementation. Excuses only highlight a weakening resolve. Allowing other priorities to set aside your well-laid plans.

In the business world some people refer to this as failure to implement (FTI).

So, where to start? Where is the low hanging fruit? When and where do you plan to start work on accelerating your profit improvement? What are you going to do differently? Where can you proactively adapt and develop the business?

While reading this book have you thought about your ability to implement change? Maybe there are issues with one or two people in the firm who might have a different view from you. Maybe they have a different agenda. The key is to start changing what is in your sphere of influence. Increasing time on. Increasing visible time. Reducing write-downs. Delivering more extension services to clients. Winning better clients.

It is important to avoid setting the bar too high and inviting failure into your profit improvement plans.

There is an old management adage that tells us that we should 'eat the elephant chunk by chunk'. Why not develop a 12-month and then a two-year plan? Make sure you develop a plan in bite size chunks.

The key to avoiding FTI? Don't over commit yourself otherwise you may under deliver. On the other hand this has to be balanced with the need to add in some S T R E T C H into your management decisions. Remember that accounting firm management tends to operate in a reactive arena while what needs to happen is to move step-by-step to take control and be as pro active as possible.

Here is a challenging one liner that always has seminar attendees taking note – and not necessarily agreeing…

> The people in your firm people are not the problem – it is the systems and processes that need fixing not the people.

I recall attending a conference in the USA when one of the speakers was talking about how to help clients with increasing their profitability. I cannot recall the detail of what he said but I will never forget the message he kept repeating.

> *"It's all about implementation."*
> Dave Krajanowski, Singer Lewack, Los Angeles

SOME KEYS FOR GAINING CONSENSUS

Your ability to gain owner-wide consensus will depend on your situation. A sole practitioner will have far less need for getting others on board than a newly appointed partner. However, there cannot be many who do not wish to see results accelerating in an upward direction.

This final chapter seems to be the one with adages and one-liners so here is another impactful adage with which you may be familiar. "If you keep on doing what you have been doing you will keep on getting what you have been getting."

How does that feel?

Remember your firm is the firm's best client. If you do not look after this client you will be unable to serve the other clients to the best of your ability and in accordance with the needs of your clients.

Yes, we live in an era where there is change around the corner seemingly every week.

> Yes, change is a challenge, but NOT changing is also a challenge.

The 'product' life cycle for compliance services is certainly not in the 'growing' phase of the bell curve while you will have your own view as to where they are positioned on the 'aging' curve.

If you are a firm owner aged under 50 you will definitely be well aware of the need to develop new services – these are after all likely to form a big part in your own financial success. If you are over 55 you may well (although I understand you may see this differently) have circled a date on your calendar when going into the office is not the first call at the beginning of each day. My encouragement to you is to release and empower the younger generation. The profession has probably been good to you. But now you recognise the challenge of change on your firm in the future. One day you will leave the firm and withdraw your capital account; you may even have an entitlement to some return for the value of the business. I consulted many years ago with Reeves & Neylan in Kent, UK. I watched as the firm changed its managing partner. They took the decision to skip a couple of generations and appointed one of the younger partners to lead the firm. The move was a good one. Clive Stevens was an excellent choice as managing partner as that firm benefited from unleashing the power of the younger generation.

SEVEN IMPLEMENTATION KEYS

If you in a partnership and wish to gain consensus you will probably have already started developing thoughts to integrate into a plan. Does it include:

1 **Creating** a strategy paper on the firm's future development options. Services. Technology. Profit Improvement. And so on.

2 **Recommending** the Double Your Income book or my audio-based version (complete with manual) to your co-owners so they can develop their own thinking alongside listening to your ideas. This is a key step in helping make 'your ideas, their ideas.' Ownership of change management programs is important. Where ownership and motivation exists there is a coalescence of purpose.

3 **Milestones.** When will the task be started? When finished? What results do you wish to achieve?

Your plans should include agreeing the dates to review progress and ensure the plan is progressing appropriately.

4 **Management roles.** Every team needs to ensure that member roles are clear. Team roles normally revolve around doers, deciders and experts. Terms that are self-explanatory I trust. If not, the Internet has much that can be studied when it comes to TBDM (Team Based Decision Making).

5 **Broadcast.** How will you communicate decisions and change plans? How will you articulate the context of change?

6 **Armouring.** What monitoring systems are appropriate to ensure that this improvement is institutionalised? You don't wish to make a gain and then lose

it along the way. Change must be sustainable otherwise change management programs can become somewhat discredited and people use past failings as an excuse for not making change.

7 **Accountability.** Do you have a process for accountability? This is often missing in accounting firms with firm owners acting as silos. Having an accountability buddy is about enlisting help, encouragement and good advice.

KPIs AND VISION NAVIGATION

We have considered already the principle of KPIs, but what are your practice management KPIs?

One of my mentors, Gerry Faust, taught me about 25 years ago that you can manage any business by managing just five numbers. *"The trick is to work out what the numbers are, whether they should go up or down and who is responsibility for each number,"* Gerry taught me.

As I was managing my accountancy business at the time I decided to accept Gerry's counsel. But, which KPIs should I monitor? I decided that I would not select any number that appeared in the profit and loss account or balance sheet – to me that was far too obvious and not overly interesting. Instead I selected numbers that were interesting to manage and would drive performance in the right direction. These were my KPIs:

Monthly:

1. Number of client meetings
2. Number of meetings with referral sources
3. Chargeable hours
4. Total hours

Working capital management:

5. Percentage of lock up to income

Managing my life by monitoring these numbers was fun and motivating – and yes, profit increased.

Vision navigation

So much of life is on the computer. Turn the computer off and the screen goes blank. I have always either used a flip chart or white board to write up my KPIs – in doing so the key numbers I wished to manage were always visible – to me and everyone else who comes into my office.

FINALLY...

With that, I will leave you to conclude your final thoughts arising from this book. Remember, I am a consultant and that I am usually only about 65 per cent correct! You are not required to agree with everything you have read. However, along this journey I hope this book will have challenged you in some areas, surprised you in others and motivated you from time to time.

Don't allow disagreement on any points to dismiss some of the other propositions. Surely that could not be a good thing?

Can you really double your income and when? That is up to you; I accept that it depends on your current level of profitability. This chapter alone provides a framework for you to decide how you are doing.

I highly recommend visiting the shop on my website. It does not matter where you are based these low cost but high impact training solutions represent great firm-wide training.

If you wish to make contact please do so by email to: mark@marklloydbottom.com

I trust the ideas you think will really work become your own – do not think you need to give me credit for any success you achieve – that is for you and your close ones to celebrate.

In my garden I have two very large oak trees. Once they were nothing other than tiny acorns. May you have success in planting these small ideas and may your practice grow into a mighty oak tree.

By the way as a post script just in case I left you hanging a little earlier in this chapter – did I become financially independent by 55? About 5 years earlier! Have I ever doubled my income? Yes.

QUESTIONS TO ASK YOURSELF

1

Do you have a marketing plan that is working?
If not, how will you improve it?

2

How much will you invest in marketing. Finance? Time?

3

What are your targets for new clients and
new engagements from current clients?

> **GOOD** BUSINESS **PLANNING** IS NINE PARTS **EXECUTION**
> FOR **EVERY** ONE PART **STRATEGY**.
>
> **TIM BERRY**

DOUBLE YOUR INCOME

PRACTICE MANAGEMENT ACADEMY
MARK'S PORTFOLIO OF TRAINING PROGRAMS

DOUBLE YOUR INCOME

This seminar focuses on laying the foundations that will enable you to maximise your profitability potential.

CONTENT INCLUDES

- How one firm increased realisation from 65% to 85% in six months
- How one London-based firm increased profits by over 100% in less than a year
- Key ways to get more chargeable hours without more overtime
- An essential future accounting firm model
- Learn the lessons from the eight ladders of success and avoid the eight ladders of complacency
- Learn how to massively eliminate time on jobs
- Essential keys in strategic planning
- Marketing –forward to some great basics
- How to bill more for the same work
- New twenty first century pricing strategies
- How to increase your minimum tax return fees
- How to increase profitability of serving existing clients
- Six steps to increasing client loyalty
- Effective strategies for gaining new clients
- Key laser like metrics that will enable you to manage smarter – rather than harder

 FIRM OWNERS

160+ PAGE MANUAL AND 3 POWER-PACKED CDs

Order your copy from **marklloydbottom.com**

DOUBLE YOUR INCOME

UPGRADE

This is a comprehensive one-on-one firm owner/prospective firm owner training programme.

CONTENT INCLUDES

THE MARKETPLACE
Exploring threats and opportunities
What successful firm owners are doing
FIRM PROFITABILITY
Exploring how the accounting firm can increase profitability
CLIENT SERVICE
The power of client meetings including the essential client meetings
How to personally deliver outstanding client service –
and derive greater job satisfaction
BILLING
How to discuss prices with clients – avoiding the trap of under billing
JOB PROFITABILITY
The essential ways to drive efficiency and improve job profitability
SELF MANAGEMENT
Benchmarking and KPIs that drive results
ADVISORY SKILLS
Essential [new] skills for giving business advice (4 hours):
Understanding and engaging with the four roles of management
The lifecycle of a business
Questions that open up the client to want more from you
MARKETING
Mind the gap – How to build valuable personal relationships
Personal marketing that guarantees to win new business
STAFF
Improving one-on-one staff management
IMPLEMENTATION
Developing the personal plan

- FIRM OWNERS
- ONE-ON-ONE PARTNER TRAINING
- FUTURE PARTNER TRAINING

45 CHAPTERS AND
TRAINING FILMS
(TOTAL ABOUT 9 HOURS)

Order your copy from **marklloydbottom.com**

DOUBLE YOUR INCOME

DEEPER: ADVANCED PRACTICE MANAGEMENT STRATEGIES

Deeper is a comprehensive programme designed to enlighten and empower you to exponentially improve what and how you manage. In so doing this programme will help you to improve profitability, reduce lock up to 15%, and achieve better firm-wide results.

CONTENT INCLUDES

- Calculate the financial cost of poor service
- Calculate the financial value of delivering outstanding service
- Learn from our four quality case studies
- Some essential client care KPIs - follow these and client service WILL improve
- Over 100 service-opening questions that will help lay your clients problems out in front of them
- Over 35 services you can deliver to your business clients
- The advanced LUBRM model and how to 'better manage the gap'
- How to downsize your lock up to 15% and have your clients welcome the change in your billing practices
- More than 25 essential benchmarks – compare your firm
- Insights for managing partners
- All of my key notes from attending management conferences for 25 years
- How to build your relationships and the firm's reputation
- Essential core marketing strategies that will deliver new business

PLUS – Chapters from more than 10 leading consultants covering such topics as profit sharing, negotiating skills, lessons from the best of the best, bringing on your talent and research-proven steps to excellence.

 FIRM OWNERS

> INCLUDES 3 CDs, 1 DVD, 200+ PAGE FULL COLOUR MANUAL, 3 SAMPLE SERVICE CARDS FOR YOUR FIRM TO ADAPT, AND MARK LLOYDBOTTOM'S BOOK RECOMMENDATIONS

Order your copy from **marklloydbottom.com**

DEFINING EDGE

Defining Edge is the first of Mark's two-part Accounting Firm Management Training Programmes for Firm Owners.

CONTENT INCLUDES

- Our LUBRM accounting firm model – how you can increase profitability
- Your personal development plan – the challenge and opportunity
- Delivering outstanding client service pays – turn your clients into powerful advocates
- Powering up your client planning meetings
- Enhancing the value of what you deliver
- The iceberg and rear view mirror models
- Why quality doesn't cost – it pays big dividends
- Billing myths – don't get caught out
- Improve utilisation - time on can increase
- Increase realisation or maybe reduce - and still increase profits!
- 10 ways to improve billing
- How to minimise write downs - a powerful case study
- How guerrilla billing reduces lock up
- The power of the 85% rule
- Marketing – what to make sure you do to win new clients
- How to build your relationships and the firm's reputation
- Essential core marketing strategies that will deliver new business

 FIRM OWNERS

> **INCLUDES A 160-PAGE COACHING MANUAL AND EITHER 6 CDs OR DVDs**

Order your copy from **marklloydbottom.com**

POWER UP YOUR GROSS MARGIN

This programme is based on my work with accounting firms over the last few years. It unlocks the secrets of how you can improve your gross margin on your jobs. Discover the steps you can take to improve profitability and how to eliminate some of your lost, non-chargeable time.

CONTENT INCLUDES

- What to monitor and manage to improve profits
- Gap management – managing what you can't see results in big dividends
- The powerful impact of client visible time
- How to get 1200 chargeable hours or more a year
- How to reduce write-downs
- Twelve lessons I learned from managers and how they impact your firm
- Fifteen strategies you can use to improve margin
- How to get paid in your client's financial year
- How to gain client approval for fees

✓ FIRM OWNERS   ✓ STAFF TRAINING

TWO-PART CD AND 64 PAGE MANUAL

Order your copy from **marklloydbottom.com**

DELIVERING OUTSTANDING CLIENT SERVICE

This two-part DVD training programme and manual provides a comprehensive overview of the power and potential of focusing on improving client service. Clients are the lifeblood of your business. Join Mark for a transfusion and powerful lessons that really will deliver outstanding service to you and your team.

CONTENT INCLUDES

- The cost of poor service and the reward of being outstanding
- Escalate your performance and improve your client report card
- The power of leveraging client meetings and how to do it
- Learn from one of the UK's most successful independent car dealerships
- Learn some innovative ideas from a self styled crazy New Zealand dentist
- Some insightful and highly impactful client care KPIs

✓ FIRM OWNERS   ✓ STAFF TRAINING

84 PAGE MANUAL AND TWO TRAINING DVDs

Order your copy from **marklloydbottom.com**

BETTER BILLING.
BETTER COLLECTIONS.
LOWER LOCK UP. GUARANTEED.

This two-part DVD training programme and manual provides insights into the major 21st century changes that are impacting the profession today. These changes are occurring in other businesses – now it's the turn of accountants.

CONTENT INCLUDES

- An in depth look at an insightful accounting firm financial model
- Dispelling the anchor of billing myths
- How to downsize your lock up (debtors and work in progress)
- New billing and collection horizons – start sooner rather than later.
- Discussing prices with clients – an end to low balling now
- Taking action and getting the desired results

 FIRM OWNERS   ✓ STAFF TRAINING

80 PAGE MANUAL AND TWO TRAINING DVDs

Order your copy from **marklloydbottom.com**

Lightning Source UK Ltd.
Milton Keynes UK
UKOW07f2132300616

277390UK00004B/77/P